Diving & Snorkeling
Hawaii

Casey & Astrid Witte Mahaney

LONELY P   S
Melbourne •   is

Diving & Snorkeling Hawaii
- A Lonely Planet Pisces Book

1st Edition
February, 2000

Published by
Lonely Planet Publications
192 Burwood Road, Hawthorn, Victoria 3122, Australia

Other offices
150 Linden Street, Oakland, California 94607, USA
10A Spring Place, London NW5 3BH, UK
1 rue du Dahomey, 75011 Paris, France

Photographs
All photographs by Casey & Astrid Witte Mahaney
unless otherwise noted

Front cover photograph
Snorkeler with lined and raccoon butterflyfish and
    Moorish idols, by Casey & Astrid Witte Mahaney

Back cover photographs
Spanish dancer emerges at night,
    by Casey & Astrid Witte Mahaney
Mount Haleakala at sunrise with the Big Island in the
    background, by Andrew Sallmon
Diver explores porthole of YO-257 wreck near Waikiki,
    by Casey & Astrid Witte Mahaney

The images in this guide are available for licensing
from Lonely Planet Images
email: lpi@lonelyplanet.com.au

ISBN 1 86450 090 5

text & maps © Lonely Planet 2000
photographs © photographers as indicated 2000
dive site maps are Transverse Mercator projection

Printed by H&Y Printing Ltd., Hong Kong

Contents

Maui County Dive Sites   82

Maui   85

Molokini Crater   90

Kahoolawe   95

Lanai   96

Molokai   102

Authors

Casey & Astrid Witte Mahaney

Casey and Astrid Witte Mahaney have lived in Hawaii and on other Pacific Islands for more than 15 years. They are internationally published photojournalists who specialize in underwater photography, and have authored five marine life identification guides and numerous scuba travel and destination guides. Having introduced thousands of divers to the intricacies of Pacific reefs, they now cater to sophisticated dive travelers and underwater photographers through an array of services, including escorted tours to exotic destinations.

From the Authors

A variety of people and organizations helped make this guide as complete and up-to-date as possible through their support and contributions of knowledge, expertise, dive vessels and accommodations. A special thanks to: Roy Esmailzadeh, John Connery and Rich Kersten of Sea Paradise on the Big Island; Brian of Pacific Diving Adventures on Oahu; Amy Stephenson and Erik Stein of Extended Horizons on Maui; Kent Brackman and Debbie Glover of Midway Sport Diving; Dr. John E. Randall of the Bishop Museum on Oahu; Linda Bail from Bubbles Below on Kauai; Tom Curley; and Fuji USA.

Photography Notes

Underwater, Casey and Astrid use a variety of cameras and formats. For macro and close-up photography they use the Nikon 8008s and N90s fitted with either a 105mm or 60mm lens in an Ikelite housing. For wide-angle photography they prefer to shoot with 20mm and 14mm lenses in a Nexus housing, or utilize the Nikonos III and V cameras with a 15mm lens. Topside, they work with their Nikon cameras and a wide variety of lenses, including zoom lenses. They prefer Fujichrome slide films such as Velvia, Provia and Sensia II for their brilliant color saturation.

Contributing Photographers

Most of the photographs in this book were taken by Casey and Astrid Witte Mahaney. Thanks also to Andrew Sallmon, Lee Foster and Beverly Factor for their photo contributions.

From the Publisher

This first edition was published in Lonely Planet's U.S. office under the guidance of Roslyn Bullas, the "Divemaster" of Pisces Books. From the coral-encrusted Fish Tank, Sarah Jane "Sunfish" Hawkins edited the text and photos with editorial help from Deb Miller and Ben Greensfelder. "Super Grouper" Emily Douglas designed the cover, and David Van Ness designed the book's interior, assisted by Emily. Navigating nautical charts were cartographers Patrick Bock, Guphy, and Mary Hagemann, who created the maps, and Alex Guilbert, who supervised map production. Bill Alevizon reviewed the marine life sections for scientific accuracy. Portions of the text were adapted from Lonely Planet's *Hawaii*. Thanks also to Ken Nichols of North Shore Diving (Oahu) for his contributions to the "Conservation & Awareness" section.

Lonely Planet Pisces Books

Lonely Planet acquired the Pisces line of diving and snorkeling books in 1997. The series is being developed and substantially revamped over the next few years. We welcome your comments and suggestions.

Pisces Pre-Dive Safety Guidelines

Before embarking on a scuba diving, skin diving or snorkeling trip, carefully consider the following to help ensure a safe and enjoyable experience:

- Possess a current diving certification card from a recognized scuba diving instructional agency (if scuba diving)
- Be sure you are healthy and feel comfortable diving
- Obtain reliable information about physical and environmental conditions at the dive site (e.g., from a reputable local dive operation)
- Be aware of local laws, regulations and etiquette about marine life and environment
- Dive at sites within your experience level; if possible, engage the services of a competent, professionally trained dive instructor or divemaster

Underwater conditions vary significantly from one region, or even site, to another. Seasonal changes can significantly alter site and dive conditions. These differences influence the way divers dress for a dive and what diving techniques they use.

There are special requirements for diving in any area, regardless of location. Before your dive, ask about environmental characteristics that can affect your diving and how trained local divers deal with these considerations.

Warning & Request

Things change—dive site conditions, regulations, topside information. Nothing stays the same for long. Your feedback on this book will be used to help update and improve the next edition. Excerpts from your correspondence may appear in *Planet Talk*, our quarterly newsletter, or *Comet*, our monthly email newsletter. Please let us know if you do not want your letter published or your name acknowledged.

Correspondence can be addressed to:
Lonely Planet Publications
Pisces Books
150 Linden Street
Oakland, CA 94607
email: pisces@lonelyplanet.com

Introduction

Hawaii is one of the world's favorite vacation destinations and its warm tropical water is just one of its greatest draws. From the island chain's high mountains to its ocean floor, you will find richness and diversity beyond compare. The people are as diverse and as welcoming as the land. As a transportation hub of the Pacific, Hawaii has attracted immigrants from the east and west, melding their cultures with local Polynesian traditions into a blend as smooth as Kona coffee.

The Hawaiian Islands appeal to travelers with a variety of interests and goals. Whether you seek a week of sunshine on a deserted sandy beach or a stimulating hiking trip through verdant tropical forests, you are bound to find what you're looking for.

No visitor should miss the underwater riches found throughout the island chain. You can explore shallow bays alive with turtles and tropical fish, or investigate deeper coral walls studded with colorful crustaceans and nudibranchs. Shallow channels are home to humpback whales, while steep drop-offs and high currents attract pelagic fish.

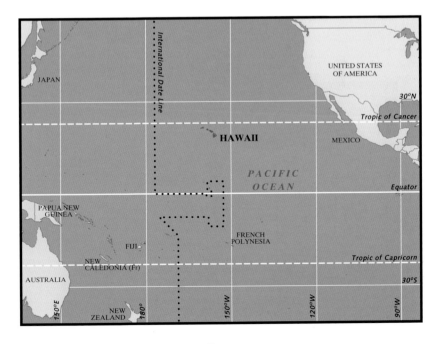

This book provides divers and snorkelers with an overview of Hawaii's unique underwater world. As you travel around this diverse island chain, you'll find many conveniently located dive sites that are easy enough for newcomers to the sport, but that still hold the interest of experienced dive enthusiasts. Many dive sites are remote and pristine, while others are current-swept and thrilling, often only suitable for advanced divers. Throughout the islands you'll have splendid visibility, find dramatic underwater lava formations and frequently encounter turtles.

Due to Hawaii's geographical isolation, a large percentage of marine life is endemic to this geologically young island group. Approximately 30% of the fish are found nowhere else in the world. Many of the corals, crustaceans and nudibranchs, as well as the Hawaiian monk seal, are also endemic to Hawaii. Divers who take the time to explore the intricacies of the reef and familiarize themselves with the local marine life will be rewarded with sightings of rare and unique fish species and colorful invertebrates. You will find that each island has its own special intrigue, both above water and below.

This book covers five principal dive regions within the island chain: **Oahu**, the **Big Island** (Hawaii), **Maui County** (including Maui, Molokini Crater, Kahoolawe, Lanai and Molokai), **Kauai & Niihau** and **Midway Islands**. The dive sites described in this guide do not constitute a comprehensive list of all dive sites in Hawaii, but were selected because they are some of the best dives in their regions, and represent each area's typical diving conditions. Each dive site description includes information to help you select dives suitable for your interests and abilities and to help you establish your dive plan. Underwater photography tips are interspersed throughout the text to help you capture your diving experience on film.

All divers will spend some time topside. The "Activities & Attractions" section provides tips on what to do on land. You'll find information about the archipelago's geological formation, history and culture in the "Overview" section, and the "Practicalities" section will help you prepare for a comfortable and enjoyable trip.

Diver descends to black coral and pyramid butterflyfish.

Overview

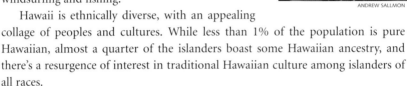

Volcanic in origin, most of the Hawaiian Islands are high and rugged, cut by spectacular, lush green gorges and valleys. Beaches range from beautiful, soft white sand to rough, dark lava rocks. The water is warm and provides opportunities for nearly endless underwater exploration and world-class surfing, windsurfing and fishing.

ANDREW SALLMON

Hawaii is ethnically diverse, with an appealing collage of peoples and cultures. While less than 1% of the population is pure Hawaiian, almost a quarter of the islanders boast some Hawaiian ancestry, and there's a resurgence of interest in traditional Hawaiian culture among islanders of all races.

These unique characteristics—the region's mild climate, varied activities and cultural attributes—have made the Hawaiian Islands one of the world's favorite tourist destinations and tourism one of the state's biggest income generators.

Geography

Hawaii is the world's most isolated archipelago, resting more than 2,400 miles (3,864km) from the nearest land mass, North America. The Hawaiian archipelago stretches across 1,523 miles (2,452km) of central Pacific Ocean (from Kure Atoll in the northwest to the Big Island in the southeast) and is the northernmost extent of Polynesia. The eight major islands—Oahu, the Big Island, Maui, Kahoolawe, Lanai, Molokai, Kauai and Niihau—have a combined land mass of 6,470 sq miles (16,757 sq km). The Northwestern Hawaiian Islands, which consist of 33 tiny atolls, are scattered across 1,000 miles (1,600km) of ocean north of Kauai.

Oahu is the gateway to the Hawaiian Islands. Its beautiful beaches and mild climate have attracted vacationers since the early 1900s. Waikiki, just south of the capital city Honolulu, still accommodates nearly half of the state's visitors.

The largest and southernmost island is Hawaii, more commonly referred to as the "Big Island" to avoid confusing it with the state as a whole. The Big Island is home to the state's highest mountain, Mauna Kea, which reaches 13,796ft (4,139m) above sea level and is the world's highest mountain when measured from the ocean floor—33,476ft (10,043m).

Maui County, north of Oahu, includes four islands and one crater—Maui, Kahoolawe, Lanai, Molokai and Molokini Crater. Maui, the most populated of these islands, is the jumping-off point for the region. The high volcanic mountains provide a stunning backdrop to its waterfalls, scenic drives and lush green landscape.

Kahoolawe is a small, uninhabited island southwest of Maui. Lanai is a fertile, teardrop-shaped island off Maui's northwest end. Molokai, just north of Lanai, is a rural, slow-paced island that is home to the world's highest sea cliffs. Molokini Crater is the tip of an extinct volcano that rises out of the water between Maui and Kahoolawe. The shallow channels between these islands are a welcome breeding and calving ground for migratory humpback whales.

Farther north is Kauai, the "Garden Island." It is famous for its lush green vegetation and the jagged splendor of the Na Pali Coast. Just west of Kauai is Niihau, the "Forbidden Island," a low-lying, windswept island that is inhabited solely by native Hawaiians and is privately owned.

Of the Northwestern Hawaiian Islands, Midway Islands are the only ones accessible to tourists. These four tiny islands—Sand, Eastern, Gooney and Spit—are part of a sheltered atoll and marine preserve that is home to many animals.

Geology

The Hawaiian Islands are the tips of massive mountains, created by a crack or hot spot in the earth's mantle that has been spewing out molten rock for more than 25 million years. The hot spot is stationary, but the ocean floor, which is part of the Pacific Plate, is moving northwest at the rate of about 3 inches (8cm) a year.

As weak spots in the earth's crust pass over the hot spot, molten lava bursts through and forms underwater volcanic mountains, some of which finally emerge above the water as islands. Each new volcano eventually creeps north from the hot spot that created it. The farther the volcano is from the lava source, the lower the volcanic activity, until the volcano eventually becomes extinct.

Once volcanic activity stops, it's a downhill battle. The forces of erosion—wind, rain and waves—slowly wear away the mountains. In addition, the settling of the ocean floor causes the land to gradually recede. Thus the once-mountainous Northwestern Hawaiian Islands (the oldest in the Hawaiian chain) are now low, flat atolls that in time will be totally submerged.

Lava flows into the ocean at Hawaii Volcanoes National Park, Big Island.

The Big Island, Hawaii's southernmost island, is still in the birthing process. Its most active volcano, Kilauea, is directly over the hot spot. Since its latest eruptive phase began in 1983, Kilauea has pumped out more than 2 billion cubic yards (1.5 billion cubic meters) of lava, making this the largest known volcanic eruption in Hawaii's history.

Less than 30 miles (48km) southeast of the Big Island, a new seamount named Loihi has already built up 15,000ft (4,500m) on the ocean floor. The growing mounds of lava are expected to break the ocean surface within 10,000 years; however, if it were to get hyperactive, it could emerge within a century or two.

Hawaii's volcanoes are shield volcanoes, which form not by explosion but by slowly building up layer upon layer of lava. They rise from the sea with gentle slopes and a relatively smooth surface. It's only after eons of facing the elements that their surfaces become sharply eroded. For this reason, the Na Pali cliffs on Kauai (the oldest of the main islands) are the most jagged in Hawaii.

Hawaii's active volcanoes are Kilauea and Mauna Loa, both on the Big Island. The Big Island's Mauna Kea and Hualalai and Maui's Haleakala are dormant, with future eruptions possible. The volcanoes on all the other Hawaiian islands are considered extinct.

Due to Hawaii's young geological age, most of the reefs are coastal fringing reefs generally found adjacent to the shore. This provides divers and snorkelers with easy access to many shallow areas with good visibility.

Around the older islands to the north are more-developed barrier reefs that form as volcanic islands gradually erode and the coral around them builds up. Midway Islands, which once had a much greater land mass and now have a barrier reef, is an example of this kind of reef development.

History

Though the Hawaiian Islands are millions of years old, the first settlers arrived only 1,500 years ago. These Polynesian settlers, believed to have sailed from the Marquesas Islands, lived harmoniously until about 600 years ago when a new wave of more aggressive Tahitian immigrants arrived.

These new immigrants soon conquered the initial, more passive residents and introduced a hierarchical social system that separated

Puukohola *heiau* was built for Kamehameha's war god in 1790.

commoners from ruling chiefs and kings (called *alii* in Hawaiian). The conquerors also introduced human sacrifices to the gods and established the *kapu* system. Kapu, a complex code of behavior and social interaction, forbade commoners to eat the same food or even walk on the same ground as the alii. A commoner who crossed the shadow of a king could be put to death. Kapu also prohibited women from eating bananas, coconuts, pork and some varieties of fish. One of the Tahitian immigrants, a powerful *kahuna* (Tahitian priest), erected the first Hawaiian temples, some of which can still be seen today. These *heiau*s were generally dedicated

Traditional Hawaiian outrigger canoe.

to the god of the harvest, Lono, or the war god, Ku. It was in the *luakini heiaus*, those temples dedicated to Ku, that human sacrifices took place.

British explorer Captain James Cook chanced upon the Hawaiian Islands in 1778, after spending the better part of the decade exploring and charting the South Pacific. After a brief stay to restock his provisions, Cook continued his northbound expedition. Failing to find the fabled passage through the Arctic, he returned to Hawaii in 1779. When he sailed into the Big Island's beautiful Kealakekua Bay on January 17, he was greeted by thousands of canoes and generally treated like a god. His arrival coincided with the Makahiki Festival, a four-month-long event of games, festivities and peace dedicated to Lono, god of the harvest. Apparently, Cook was mistaken for this god.

The Birthplace of Global Communication

The Midway Islands were discovered in 1859 by Captain Nick Brooks of the ship *Gambia*. In 1903 President Roosevelt placed the atoll under the control of the U.S. Navy. Only a few months later, the Commercial Pacific Cable Company established a relay station on the atoll, allowing President Roosevelt to send the first "around the world" cable message via Midway.

In 1941 the U.S. Naval Air Station Midway was commissioned and remained in operation until September 1993, when the facility was officially closed. The navy has since transferred control of the islands to the U.S. Fish and Wildlife Service, which initiated and continues habitat restoration and species-management projects.

When Cook returned a few weeks later to repair a broken mast, the Makahiki Festival had ended. Cook's timing and the conditions of his return proved inauspicious. A variety of misunderstandings and a series of unfortunate events finally resulted in a group of native Hawaiians stabbing Cook to death. Cook's crew was able to safely return home with charts, drawings and stories of their travels. The western world would soon recognize the vast bounty of Hawaii.

In 1819 the first missionaries and whaling ships arrived,

both quickly flourishing. By 1855 the whaling industry had reached its peak, but the need for whale oil soon declined due to the increased use of petroleum oil. To compensate for this economic shift, Hawaii developed its agricultural industries.

As native Hawaiians were decimated by diseases introduced by immigrants from Europe and the Americas, new labor forces were imported from China, Japan, the Philippines and Portugal, setting the foundation for a Hawaii that would be known as the cultural "melting pot of the Pacific."

The U.S. annexed Hawaii in 1898, attracted not so much by its tropical climate as by its strategic location halfway between the U.S. and its new possession, the Philippines. While Hawaii's economy boomed during the early 20th century as a result of the emerging sugar and pineapple industries, the U.S. established military bases throughout the islands. Both Oahu and the Midway Islands were used as operations bases and became integral defense points. The U.S. was jolted into WWII when a wave of Japanese bombers attacked Pearl Harbor on December 7, 1941. The U.S. fleet was caught by surprise—more than 20 U.S. ships and 347 aircraft were sunk, damaged or destroyed and 2,500 people were killed. Less than a year later, in July 1942, U.S. troops retaliated by thwarting a Japanese surprise attack on Midway, stopping their further advancement into Pacific territories.

When Hawaii assumed U.S. statehood in 1959, commercial development and urbanization of the islands intensified. Since that time, agricultural industries have all but vanished, and tourist enterprises have filled the economic gap. Tourism now represents the largest sector of Hawaii's economy, accounting for approximately 30% of the state's income. Many tourists visit Hawaii to enjoy the island chain's unique marine life, and there are more than a hundred diving and snorkeling services catering to them.

Waikiki has been Hawaii's premier tourist destination since the early 1900s.

LEE FOSTER

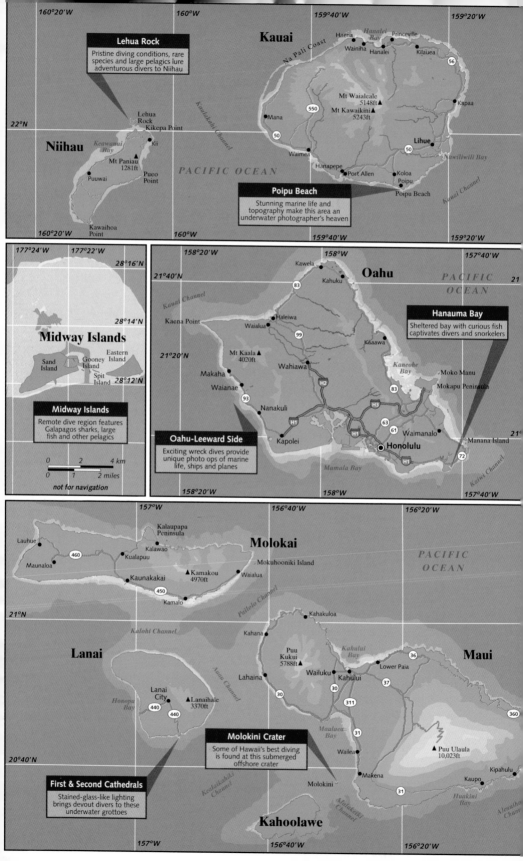

Kauai

Haena
Wainiha
Hanalei
Princeville
Kilauea
Hanalei Bay
Na Pali Coast
56
Kapaa
Mt Waialeale 5148ft▲
Mt Kawaikini▲ 5243ft
Lihue
550
Mana
50
Nawiliwili Bay
Waimea
Hanapepe
Port Allen
Koloa
Poipu
Poipu Beach
Kauai Channel

PACIFIC OCEAN

22°N

Kaulakahi Channel

Niihau

Lehua Rock
Kikepa Point
Kii
Keawanui Bay
Mt Paniau▲ 1281ft
Puuwai
Pueo Point
Kawaihoa Point

160°20'W   160°W   159°40'W   159°20'W

Midway Islands

177°24'W   177°22'W   28°16'N   28°14'N

Sand Island
Gooney Island
Eastern Island
Spit Island
28°12'N

0   2   4 km
0   1   2 miles

not for navigation

Oahu

158°20'W   158°W   157°40'W

21°40'N   21

Kawela
Kahuku
Haleiwa
Waialua
Kauai Channel
Kaena Point
99
83
Kaaawa
PACIFIC OCEAN
Mt Kaala ▲ 4020ft
Wahiawa
H2
Kaneohe Bay
Moko Manu
Mokapu Peninsula
Makaha
Waianae
93
Nanakuli
H3
63
Waimanalo
H1
61
Kapolei
H1
Honolulu
72
Manana Island
Mamala Bay
H1
21°

21°20'N

158°20'W   158°W   157°40'W

Molokai

157°W   156°40'W   156°20'W

Lauhue
Kalaupapa Peninsula
Kalawao
Kalaupapa
460
Kualapuu
Maunaloa
Mokuhooniki Island
Kaunakakai
▲ Kamakou 4970ft
Waialua
PACIFIC OCEAN
450
Kamalo
21°N

Lanai

Kalohi Channel
Pailolo Channel
Kahakuloa

Lanai City
440
440
▲ Lanaihale 3370ft
Honopu Bay
Auau Channel
Lahaina
Kahana
Puu Kukui 5788ft▲
Kahului Bay
Wailuku
Kahului
Lower Paia
36
30
30
311
37
Maalaea Bay
31

Maui

360
▲ Puu Ulaula 10,023ft
Wailea
Makena
Kipahulu
31
Kaupo
Huakini Bay

Molokini

Kealaikahiki Channel
Alalakeiki Channel
Alenuihaha Bay

Kahoolawe

20°40'N

157°W   156°40'W   156°20'W

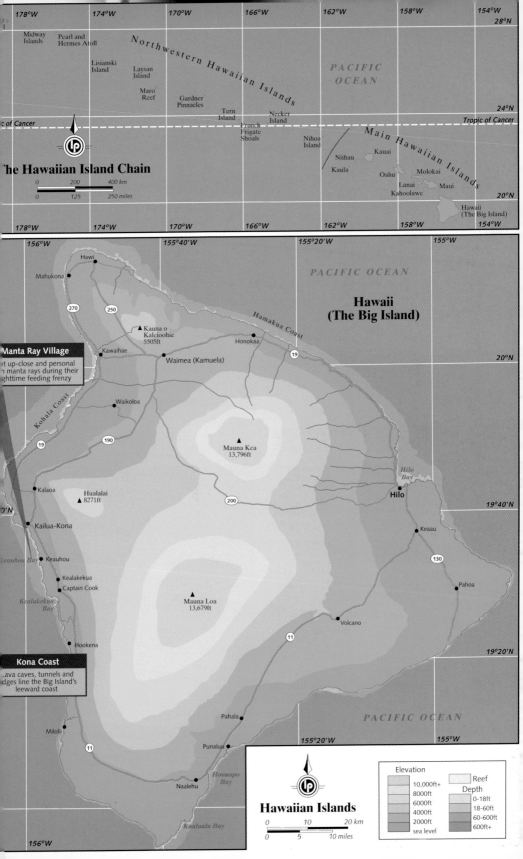

The Hawaiian Island Chain

178°W · 174°W · 170°W · 166°W · 162°W · 158°W · 154°W

28°N

Midway Islands
Pearl and Hermes Atoll
Lisianski Island
Laysan Island
Maro Reef
Gardner Pinnacles
Tern Island
Necker Island
French Frigate Shoals

Northwestern Hawaiian Islands

PACIFIC OCEAN

24°N

Tropic of Cancer — — — — — — — — — — — — Tropic of Cancer

Nihoa Island

Main Hawaiian Islands

Niihau
Kaula
Kauai
Oahu
Molokai
Lanai
Kahoolawe
Maui

20°N

Hawaii (The Big Island)

| 0 | 200 | 400 km |
| 0 | 125 | 250 miles |

178°W · 174°W · 170°W · 166°W · 162°W · 158°W · 154°W

156°W · 155°40'W · 155°20'W · 155°W

PACIFIC OCEAN

Hawaii (The Big Island)

Hawi
Mahukona
270
250
Kauna o Kaleioohie 5505ft

Hamakua Coast

Honokaa
19
Kawaihae
Waimea (Kamuela)

20°N

Manta Ray Village
…et up-close and personal
…n manta rays during their
…ghttime feeding frenzy

Waikoloa

Kohala Coast

19
190

Mauna Kea 13,796ft

Hilo Bay

Kalaoa
Hualalai 8271ft
200
Hilo

19°40'N

Kailua-Kona
Keaau
130

…eauhou Bay
Keauhou
Kealakekua
Captain Cook

Kealakekua Bay

Mauna Loa 13,679ft
Pahoa

Hookena

Volcano

Kona Coast
…ava caves, tunnels and
…dges line the Big Island's
leeward coast

11

19°20'N

Pahala

Milolii
11
Punaluu

PACIFIC OCEAN

Honuapo Bay

155°20'W · 155°W

Naalehu

Hawaiian Islands

| 0 | 10 | 20 km |
| 0 | 5 | 10 miles |

Kaalualu Bay

Elevation
10,000ft+
8000ft
6000ft
4000ft
2000ft
sea level

Reef

Depth
0-18ft
18-60ft
60-600ft
600ft+

156°W

LEE FOSTER

Practicalities

Climate

Hawaii's climate is considered one of the most pleasant in the world. It is comfortably balmy and warm year-round, with northeasterly trade winds prevailing most of the year. Average winter and summer temperatures vary by only 7°F (4°C). Near the coast, temperatures are between 68° and 83°F (20° and 28°C), though highland temperatures can be much cooler. Water temperatures range from a low of 72°F (22°C) in January to a high of 82°F (27°C) in August.

Generally, high mountains throughout the island chain block the trade winds and moisture-laden clouds that blow in from the northeast. These winds bring abundant rainfall to the windward side of the islands, while the leeward areas tend to receive only 10 to 25 inches (25 to 64cm) of rain a year. The rainiest time

Southern Winds

A special weather condition that can occur on all islands is called "kona weather" or "kona winds." (*Kona* means "leeward" in Hawaiian.) During kona weather, the winds shift from the typical northeast trade wind direction and blow instead from the south. Kona weather is fairly rare, occurring only a few days a year during the winter months. What makes it special and significant to divers is that it opens up dive sites that are inaccessible under normal (trade wind) conditions. The ocean swell patterns change at this time—snorkeling spots suddenly become surfing spots and vice versa.

Changing wind conditions can turn calm waters into turbulent swells during kona weather.

of the year for most of the islands is from December to March, except along the Kona Coast on the Big Island, which experiences its wettest season during July and August.

Midway Islands have a more seasonal climate than the rest of the island chain. Summer air temperatures are similar to the main Hawaiian islands, but winter temperatures can drop to 60°F (16°C), with strong winds that make it seem even colder. Water temperatures may reach 80°F (27°C) in August, but drop to 65°F (18°C) in January.

Language

English is the official language of Hawaii, though it is peppered with colorful Hawaiian phrases, words borrowed from the various immigrant languages, and pidgin, a modern and ever-changing local slang based on a simplified form of English. It is common to hear islanders use pidgin to communicate with each other.

The only place where Hawaiian is still the primary language is on the privately owned island of Niihau, but many Hawaiian names, words and expressions are still commonly used throughout all the islands. In fact, some 85% of all place names in Hawaii are in

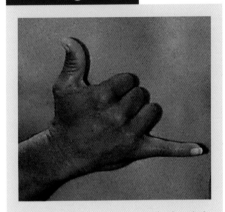

Shaka Sign

Islanders greet each other with the *shaka* sign, which is made by folding down the three middle fingers to the palm and extending the thumb and little finger. The hand is then usually held up and shaken in greeting. It's as common as waving.

Hawaiian and often have interesting translations and stories behind them. Though Hawaiian words may seem long and complicated, the written language has just 12 letters. Pronunciation and meaning are indicated through glottal stops (') and macrons (short, straight lines over some vowels), though these are often omitted in modern texts.

Getting There

Hawaii is a major transportation hub for the Pacific, connecting distant shores on all sides. Nearly all flights to Hawaii enter via the Honolulu International Airport on Oahu, which is serviced daily by major carriers from the U.S. mainland, Asia, Australia, Canada, New Zealand and the South Pacific. Some of the outer islands also have direct flights to the U.S. mainland and Asia, but these schedules are less reliable and change with demand.

Downtown Honolulu
& Chinatown

Aala Park

Foster Botanical Garden
Entrance

Chinatown Cultural Plaza

Maunakea Marketplace

Oahu Market

C H I N A T O W N

Nuuanu Stream

Hawaii Theatre

Chinatown Gateway Plaza

Cathedral of Our Lady of Peace

Honolulu Publishing

Old Honolulu Police Station

No 1 Capitol District

St Andrew's Cathedral

Washington Place

D O W N T O W N

C Brewer Building

Alexander & Baldwin Building

Bank of America Center

Aloha Tower

Dillingham Building

Grosvenor Center

Hawaiian Electric Company

YWCA

Iolani Barracks

Iolani Palace

State Capitol

Aloha Tower Marketplace

Pier 8

Falls of Clyde

Hawaii Maritime Center

Pier 6

Federal Building

Hawaii State Library

Hawaii State Office Building

Aliiolani Hale

Honolulu Hale (City Hall)

Territorial Building

Kawaiahao Church

Prince Kuhio Federal Building

Cemetery

Cemetery

Mission Houses Museum

Restaurant Row

Honolulu Harbor

To Airport

To Waikiki and Ala Moana Beach

To Royal Mausoleum

Nimitz Hwy
Iwilei Rd
N King St
N Hotel St
N Beretania St
Pauahi St
Maunakea St
Smith St
Nuuanu Ave
River St
N Kukui St
Vineyard Blvd
Nuuanu Ave
Kukui St
N Beretania St
Queen Emma St
Richards St
S Hotel St
S Beretania St
S King St
Punchbowl St
Merchant St
Queen St
Fort St Mall
Main St
Gravier
Kekaulike St
Alakea St
Bishop St
Chaplain Lane
Bethel St
Fort St Mall
Ala Moana Blvd
Aloha Tower Dr
Halekauwila St
Mililani St
Pedestrian Mall
Kinau St
Mission Lane
South St
Keawe St
Pohukaina St
Reed Lane
Cooke St
Coral St
Queen St
College Walk
Aala St

0   75   150 m
0   75   150 yards

Gateway City - Honolulu

Honolulu, with a population of about 400,000, is the state's capital and center of business, culture and politics. Honolulu International Airport and Honolulu Harbor are Hawaii's busiest ports. Since the late 1700s, Honolulu has provided a safe harbor for international travelers, many of whom have made this their home. Honolulu's ethnic diversity can be seen on every corner. Its eclectic mix of sleek high-rises and Victorian-era buildings combine well with the Spanish-style City Hall, the missionary churches and the Royal Palace. Many interesting and historic sites are within walking distance of each other. Though the greater Honolulu area has seen tremendous growth throughout the 20th century, the downtown area near the harbor remains the heart of the city.

Just south of downtown Honolulu is Waikiki, a 1½-mile-long stretch of golden beach lined by countless hotels, restaurants, bars and shops. As Hawaii's first tourist destination, Waikiki still accommodates nearly half of the state's visitors.

Getting Around

The usual method for traveling from one island to another is by plane. (Boat or ferry services are not normally available between islands.) Aloha Airlines and Hawaiian Airlines are the two major inter-island carriers that service the five major airports—

Inter-Island Airlines	
Aloha Airlines	(808) 484-1111
Hawaiian Airlines	(808) 838-1555
Island Air	(808) 484-2222
Trans Air	(808) 836-8080
Phoenix Air	(888) 643-9291

Honolulu (on Oahu), Kona and Hilo (on the Big Island), Kahului (on Maui) and Lihue (on Kauai). Hawaiian Airlines also flies to Molokai and Lanai (in Maui County), while the small commuter airlines, Island Air and Trans Air, service the smaller airports at Waimea-Kohala (on the Big Island), Kapalua and Hana (on Maui), and Kalaupapa (on Molokai). The only flights to Midway Islands leave from Honolulu. The route is serviced by Aloha Airlines and Phoenix Air on private charter flights, both scheduled by Midway Phoenix Corporation.

To get around each of the islands, it's best to travel by rental car. Taxis can be quite costly and public transportation is limited. On Midway the best methods of transport are bicycle or golf cart. Both can be rented.

Entry

The conditions for entering Hawaii are the same as for entering any other state in the United States. U.S. citizens should carry valid photo ID. Citizens of countries that are participants in the Visa Waiver Pilot Program (VWPP) may enter the U.S. for up to 90 days with a valid passport without obtaining a visa first. (For more information about the VWPP, access http://travel.state.gov/vwpp.html.) Visitors from all other countries must have a valid passport from their home country and a valid U.S. visa (obtainable through a U.S. consulate or embassy) to enter the U.S.

Midway Islands is an unincorporated possession of the U.S., but is outside the U.S. customs service. Therefore, visitors to Midway must re-enter the U.S. through federal port facilities at the Honolulu airport. U.S. citizens need to show proof of citizenship such as a current passport, birth certificate (showing birth in the U.S.) or U.S. certificate of citizenship.

Honolulu is the gateway to the Hawaiian Islands.

Money

The U.S. dollar (US$) is the only accepted currency. All major credit cards and traveler's checks in US$ are widely accepted throughout Hawaii.

On Midway Islands, meals and accommodations are generally prepaid. You will need cash or traveler's checks in US$ for the snack shop. Credit cards are accepted only in the bar.

Tipping in Hawaii and Midway is the same as in the rest of the U.S. The standard rate for restaurant service and taxi drivers is 10 to 20%, and hotel bellhops should be given at least $1 per bag.

Time

Hawaii is just east of the international date line. When it's noon in Hawaii, it is 2pm in San Francisco, 10pm in London and 8am the next day in Sydney. Hawaii does not observe daylight saving time, so the time difference is one hour greater during those months when other countries observe daylight saving time. Being on "Hawaiian Time" means living at a very laid-back pace, though it's sometimes used as an excuse for being late.

Electricity

Electricity is the same as on the U.S. mainland: 110 volts, 60 cycles. Two-pronged flat plugs (some with a third, round grounding prong) are used. Some electronics and department stores sell voltage converters and plug adapters, but it's best to bring your own if you know that you'll need them. Remember that many strobe and flashlight battery chargers can be switched from 110 volts to 220 volts and vice versa.

Weights & Measures

The imperial system of measurement is used throughout Hawaii. Distances are in inches, feet, yards and miles. Weights are in ounces, pounds and tons. Air pressure on scuba gauges is read in pounds per square inch (PSI) and under-water depth is read in feet. See the conversion chart on the inside of the back cover for metric equivalents.

In this book, both imperial and metric measurements are given, except for specific references within the dive site descriptions, which are given in imperial units only.

What to Bring
General Supplies

A casual attitude toward dress prevails. Shorts, sandals and a T-shirt are standard throughout the islands. An aloha shirt (a colorful Hawaiian-print shirt) and lightweight slacks for men and a cotton dress for women are sufficiently dressy even for formal occasions. If you plan to travel to higher elevations, be sure to bring a sweater and raincoat. Good walking shoes are also recommended if you are visiting rocky or mountainous areas such as Hawaii Volcanoes National Park.

As in most western countries, you'll find everything you'll need on Hawaii's five main islands, though at a 25% higher cost than on the U.S. mainland. Outer islands such as Molokai and Lanai have a limited stock of retail goods, so you may want to bring your own film, batteries or other items you are particular about. It is also a good idea to bring a supply of any prescription medicine to last for the duration of your trip, though pharmacies on the main islands are readily available and well stocked.

When visiting Midway Islands, be sure to bring everything you may need, except for food items. Meals are part of your accommodations package, and snacks can be purchased at Midway's single small store. Weather conditions on Midway are slightly different than in the rest of Hawaii. A lightweight sweater, raincoat and long pants are recommended even during the summer months.

Dive-Related Equipment

Hawaii's five main islands are all well stocked with quality rental and retail equipment. However, if you are visiting in winter when water temperatures can drop below 74°F (23°C), if you tend to get cold easily or if you plan to dive a lot, bring your own 5mm wetsuit—most dive operators only rent 3mm shorty wetsuits. If you plan to purchase a warmer wetsuit when you arrive, you may be disappointed, as few shops sell 5mm suits.

Around Midway Islands, the water temperatures may be below 70°F (21°C) even as late in the year as May or June, so adequate neoprene protection is essential. A full selection of quality rental gear, including 7mm wetsuits, is available, though in limited sizes. Be sure to reserve your rental equipment in advance or bring your own.

Underwater Photography

On Oahu, E-6 processing is available at retail stores such as Fox Photo, Light Ink and Fromes. On Maui there are also a variety of labs that offer fast E-6 processing service, including the Maui Custom Color Lab, Fox Photo and others. On the Big Island, currently only Zac's has one-hour E-6 processing available. On the other islands it may be more difficult to find fast processing services.

If you are looking to rent an underwater camera, you'll find that dive shops generally rent only Motomarine cameras, and not the higher-quality Nikonos V. Though you may find stores advertising Nikonos V cameras for rent, often the cameras are out being repaired. Serious underwater photographers should bring their own equipment as well as some backup supplies.

Business Hours

On all of the major islands you'll find convenience stores and some grocery stores open 24 hours a day. Drugstores usually open at 9am and close late in the evenings, with varying closing times. Tourist-oriented stores often open at 10am and close their doors at 10pm. Though most banks are open from 8:30am to 4:30pm, many offer extended service one or two days a week, and some are even open Saturdays. Automated teller machines (ATMs) can be found outside of banks and in grocery stores throughout the state.

Accommodations

Hawaii offers everything from the most elegant and luxurious resorts to simple hotels with shared bathrooms. Many dive operators offer packages in conjunction with mid- to high-priced hotels or condominiums. Major resorts usually have their own integrated dive operation.

Romantics can opt to stay in bed & breakfasts, which vary in price and can be found on most islands. Some B&B's even cater to divers and snorkelers.

There are also numerous public campgrounds on the islands, but few privately owned campgrounds are available. Though theft and violent crime are not common, campers—especially those traveling alone—should be cautious. Campgrounds that are well established, have caretakers, and attract other campers are good bets.

On Midway Islands, the only accommodations available are the former military bachelor-officers' quarters constructed in the mid-1950s. All guest rooms have been renovated and are spacious and comfortable. Reservations must be prepaid through Midway Phoenix Corporation. See "Listings" for details.

Dining & Food

Hawaii offers an array of dining options, from international gourmet cuisine to American fast food. Continental or European restaurants are found in most hotels, and Asian restaurants are common. Most restaurants offer at least a few fresh seafood dishes.

The Hawaiian *luau* is a buffet-style meal that features *kalua,* a whole pig that is cooked in an *imu* (an oven dug into the ground). Tourists can participate in a commercial version of this traditional celebration.

The "plate lunch" is popular with the locals and consists of two scoops of rice, a scoop of macaroni salad and a generous portion of teriyaki chicken, *kalua* pig, Spam or other meat dish. Fish, pork and taro wrapped in a *ti* leaf is known as *laulau.* Taro is also used to make *poi,* a paste pounded from cooked taro and water. *Pupus* is the word used for appetizers, such as *poke* (marinated raw fish), *limu* (seaweed) salad, sashimi or anything else used as hors d'oeuvres.

There are three restaurants on Midway Islands: the Galley serves international, cafeteria-style dishes, the Clipper House Restaurant serves gourmet-type meals, and the All Hands Club bar and grill serves burgers and beverages.

Shopping

With Hawaii's endless souvenir options you'll be able to shop to your heart's content. You'll find everything from T-shirts and plastic hula dancers to dolphin statues and beautiful wooden bowls hand-crafted from native wood. On Midway Islands (an exception to many of Hawaii's general rules) there is little to buy except for postcards and T-shirts.

Black-coral jewelry and shell ornaments are found in most tourist shops. It is illegal in Hawaii to remove stony coral from the reefs, but black coral is fair game throughout the state. Before purchasing black-coral products, understand that live black coral is harvested to create jewelry, resulting in the depletion of this stunning coral. The same considerations must be contemplated when purchasing shell products. Most shell products are not made from shells that were washed

A local works on a traditional Hawaiian sculpture.

up on the beach, but rather from live animals taken from the reefs. Buying such products only encourages the depletion of the oceans' natural resources, and lessens the beauty and biodiversity of the reefs.

LEE FOSTER

Activities & Attractions

Hawaii's beautiful beaches and varied diving aren't the only things that have made it a popular tourist destination. The islands offer activities that are suitable for the entire family or challenging enough for the most experienced adventurer, and there is something to fit all budgets. All beaches are public and there are no entrance fees. Resorts that are located on the beach are required to provide public access and free parking. There are no fees for state parks, including historical sites and other attractions located within the state parks. National parks, such as Hawaii Volcanoes National Park on the Big Island, do charge entrance fees. The following activities and attractions represent some of the best possibilities.

Oahu

Oahu is world famous for its **surfing** and Waikiki Beach is where it all began. The surf conditions here offer ample opportunities for beginners; rental boards and lessons are readily available. Another popular surf spot is just off Diamond Head, where large swells roll in during the summer months. The area is accessible via Diamond Head Road. You can view the surf from several lookouts along the road. In the winter months, Oahu's north shore turns into a surfer's heaven. The waves can be huge and are definitely only suitable for experts. Here you'll find famous surf spots such as Banzai Pipeline, Sunset Beach and Waimea Bay.

On Oahu's north shore you'll find the **Waimea Valley Adventure Park** (just across the highway from Waimea Bay Beach Park) in the beautiful, lush Waimea Valley. This commercial operation boasts an array of fun activities including

Riding Oahu's big waves

horseback riding, kayaking and **ATV tours.** To reach **Waimea Falls**, you can take the ¾-mile- (1.2km-) long path that meanders through the botanical gardens or, if you prefer, you can take a short tram ride that winds its way to the waterfall.

Sea Life Park is just north of Makapuu Point on the windward side of Oahu's southeast tip. This large commercial affair boasts a huge 300,000-gallon (1,137,000-liter) tank displaying sharks, rays, moray eels and turtles. There is also an outdoor exhibit featuring several monk seals and two amphitheaters where jumping dolphins and waddling penguins perform their tricks.

The **Waikiki Aquarium** is the third oldest public museum in the U.S. The small building was recently entirely renovated. Of special interest are the shark, monk seal, nautilus and seahorse exhibits. There are also nice displays of black-coral forests and rare endemic species that even divers seldom encounter.

The **Bishop Museum** in Honolulu is one of the Pacific's main natural-history museums and its collection features several compelling exhibits and galleries that document Polynesian and Melanesian cultures.

More than 1.5 million people "remember Pearl Harbor" each year with a visit to the **USS** *Arizona* **Memorial**. Operated by the National Park Service, the memorial is Hawaii's most visited attraction. The visitors center is open from 7:30am to 5pm daily except some holidays. Admission to the museum, the documentary film and the trip to the offshore memorial is free.

The Attack of Pearl Harbor

On December 7, 1941, a wave of Japanese bombers attacked Pearl Harbor, jolting the U.S. into WWII. The attack caught the U.S. fleet by surprise, and the toll it took on American and Japanese lives was tragic. During the few hours that the battle took place, 18 ships sank, nearly 200 airplanes were destroyed and more than 2,500 lives were lost. The USS *Arizona* was the single greatest loss, holding 1,177 sailors when it took a direct hit and sank in less than nine minutes.

Big Island

If you go to the Big Island, you must visit **Hawaii Volcanoes National Park**. The park's scenery is awesome, with dozens of craters and cinder cones. The centerpiece of the park is the steaming Kilauea Caldera (the sunken center of Kilauea Volcano), which is said to be the home of Pele, the Hawaiian goddess of volcanoes. Kilauea's southeast rift has been actively flowing since 1983. To obtain information on the volcano's current status and the best observation point to watch the lava flow, you can contact the park's 24-hour hot line at ☎ (808) 985-6000. The caldera is about a 2½-hour drive from Kailua-Kona (96 miles or 155km) or 40 minutes from Hilo (30 miles or 48km). It is another hour down to where you can see lava flowing into the ocean, so be sure to allow ample time for the trip.

Mauna Kea's summit at 13,796ft (4,139m) has some of the best **stargazing** conditions in the world. With its generally cloudless nights and clear, dry air, it is no surprise that the largest collection of state-of-the-art telescopes is assembled here. The visitors center offers free summit tours on the weekends but you need to provide your own transportation to the summit. Paradise Safaris offers guided tours that begin at sunset and include transportation and stargazing from their own telescope. Waipio Valley Shuttle offers daytime tours that include transportation and an observatory visit.

In ancient Hawaiian times commoners who broke a *kapu* (law) were hunted down and killed. Only those who were able to reach *Puuhonua o Honaunau* (**Place of Refuge**) before being captured were spared their lives. Today, Place of Refuge is a national historical park that encompasses ancient temples and a variety of other old Hawaiian buildings.

At 1 mile (1.6km) wide and nearly 6 miles (9.6km) deep, **Waipio Valley** is the largest of the seven dramatic amphitheater valleys on the windward side of the Kohala Mountains. The scenery here is spectacular, with cliffs that reach heights of up to 2,000ft (600m) wrapping around the valley. The lush green valley consists of tangled jungle vegetation, flower gardens, taro patches and stunning waterfalls. The narrow, steep road that winds down to Waipio is only accessible to hikers or four-wheel-drive vehicles. This spectacular valley is well worth visiting, and a variety of tours are available.

The long flipper of a humpback whale emerges from the water.

On the Big Island, **whale watching** is not just offered during humpback season: several charter operators run whale watching tours year-round. Although the humpbacks are the highlight of whale watching trips during the winter months, other whales—such as sperm whales and pilot whales—can be found in the deep waters farther offshore.

The Big Island, with vast pasturelands and upcountry forests, has a rich ranching history and is also home to the largest privately owned ranch in the U.S. There are a variety of outfitters that offer **horseback riding**. Trail rides range from scenic mountain rides or explorations of the various ranches to trots through the spectacular Waipio Valley.

Some of the world's best **deep-sea fishing** is found along the Kona Coast, with Kona holding most of the world's records for Pacific blue marlin. Kona's shores drop off quickly into deep blue water, giving fast access to large game fish. The large lee provided by the Big Island's massive mountains extends several miles offshore and provides ideal fishing conditions. If you are interested in deep-sea fishing, you'll find dozens of fishing charter boats offering their services.

Maui County

Maui's **Haleakala National Park** is home to the world's largest dormant volcano, Haleakala. Its summit has long been considered a natural "power point," where magnetic and cosmic forces unite. *Haleakala* means "house of the sun" in Hawaiian, and viewing the sunrise from the rim of the crater is considered a magical experience.

Mount Haleakala at sunrise, with the Big Island in the background.

One way to enjoy this daily event is to sign up for a **bicycling tour** that begins at the summit before dawn. From there you'll enjoy a 38-mile (61km) ride down-hill, dropping a total of 10,000ft (3,000m) in elevation. Haleakala National Park also has an extensive network of spectacular **hiking trails** throughout its moonlike landscape. Before you start your adventure to Haleakala, be sure to check the weather forecast. Due to the elevation, it is often cloudy or rainy and the temper-ature tends to be significantly lower than along the coast.

The **road to Hana** is regarded by many as the most beautiful drive on earth. From Kahului, the road winds past spectacular scenery of gorgeous coastal views, lush valleys, mountains and countless waterfalls and streams. Though the drive is only 50 miles (80km) long, it's not one to be rushed. The narrow highway leads you over 54 bridges and through more than 600 hairpin turns to finally bring you to the small community of Hana. Here, be sure to meet the friendly locals, or take a walk through the bamboo forest.

Each year, North Pacific humpback whales migrate from Alaska to the Hawaiian Islands. They spend each winter in Hawaii's warm waters, where they breed and bear their young. Since humpbacks like to stay in shallow water when they have newborn calves, the channels surrounding Maui tend to attract the largest numbers of whales, allowing for many outstanding **whale watching** opportunities. There are numerous charter operations that specialize in whale watching cruises, but there are also some excellent shoreline whale watching spots such as the stretches from Olowalu to Maalaea Bay and from Keawakapu Beach to Makena Beach. Divers often have the privilege of seeing whales during surface intervals, while cruising to the dive site or on rare occasions a humpback whale may be encountered during a dive.

Windsurfers brave the waves at world-famous Hookipa Beach.

Some of the world's best **windsurfing** spots are found on Maui. Hookipa Beach on the north shore is recognized as a world-class site for advanced windsurfers. Novice and intermediate windsurfers will find more suitable conditions at Spreckelsville Beach or Kanaha Beach in Kahului Bay. There are numerous shops in Kahului that rent windsurfing boards and offer lessons.

The **Maui Ocean Center** in Wailuku is a state-of-the-art aquarium featuring a 600,000 gallon (2,730,000 liter) tank that is home to tiger sharks, rays and other big fish. Marine life enthusiasts will enjoy both the indoor and outdoor displays, which introduce the Hawaiian underwater world through coral reef scenes, lava formation exhibits and deep-sea creatures. Of special interest to divers are the tanks with frogfish and garden eels, critters that are normally either well camouflaged or concealed within the reef's crevices. Visitors also learn about the Hawaiian culture and its age-old link to the sea.

Kauai & Niihau

Kayaking has become one of the most popular ways to explore some of Kauai's most remote coastal wilderness areas, such as the dramatic **Na Pali Coast** and otherwise inaccessible parts of the Huleia, Wailua and Hanalei Rivers. There are a variety of kayak outfitters that rent kayaks and offer guided tours. The advantages of a guided tour include increased safety, access to restricted natural areas and management of difficult logistics. Some operators include famous attractions such as the movie sites of *Raiders of the Lost Ark* in their guided excursions, while others specialize in honeymoon packages. Kayak Kauai is best known for their adventurous tour along the Na Pali cliffs.

If you are looking for a less active (but just as exhilarating) means to explore the Na Pali Coast, you can join one of the ocean **Zodiac safaris** or take a **helicopter ride** to marvel at the sheer cliffs and cascading waterfalls from a bird's-eye view. Any of these adventure tours will provide you with an unforgettable experience and spectacular scenery found only on Kauai.

Other ways to explore Kauai's spectacular wilderness are while **horseback riding** or on a **four-wheel-drive tour**. CJM Country Stables offers rides to secluded beaches along the southwest shore, while Princeville Ranch Stables guides riders through north Kauai's lush valleys. Kauai Mountain Tours offers a beautiful and informative four-wheel-drive mountain tour.

Often referred to as the "Grand Canyon of the Pacific," **Waimea Canyon** was created over the course of millions of years by the waters that drain from Mount Waialeale, whose summit has been called the wettest spot on earth. It receives an estimated 480 inches (1,219cm) of precipitation each year. The 2,785ft- (836m-) deep canyon provides spectacular scenery, regardless of whether you go on an extended hike into the canyon, take a walk along one of the marked trails or simply drive to one of the scenic lookouts to enjoy the spectacular view.

Bird-watching can be a rewarding experience at any of the wildlife refuges, which are home to migratory seabirds and nonmigratory endemic fowl. In the Hanalei and Huleia National Wildlife Refuges you can see endangered native species such as the Hawaiian duck, Hawaiian coot and Hawaiian stilt. Kilauea Point National Park is an excellent area to observe tropic birds, great frigates, shearwaters and other seabirds.

LEE FOSTER

Waimea Canyon is known as the "Grand Canyon of the Pacific."

You can also venture to Kauai's neighboring island **Niihau**, the "Forbidden Island," which has been privately owned by the Robinson family since 1864. Inhabited solely by native Hawaiians, the island has been entirely closed to tourism until recently, when the family began to allow a limited number of tourists to visit and view the island via **helicopter tours** from Kauai. You can join a three-hour tour to a remote beach, but are not likely to catch even a glimpse of a Hawaiian settlement or any of the 200 residents. If the idea of **hunting Polynesian boar and wild sheep** appeals to you, Niihau Safaris also offers hunting trips to the outer reaches of Niihau.

Midway Islands

Most nature lovers are attracted to Midway by the 16 species of seabirds that use the atoll as their nesting site. When you are not diving, you are automatically **bird-watching**, since birds are virtually everywhere. There are more than half a million Laysan albatross (white gooney bird) breeding pairs, comprising 70% of the world's population of the species. Laysan albatross mate for life. Each pair builds its nest in November for a single egg laid in December. In March the eggs hatch and by August the chicks have learned to fly. Both parents and chicks leave by mid-August, but they return in October to start the process again. Since albatross nest on the ground, the entire atoll is covered with birds from mid-October until mid-August.

In addition to Laysan albatross, visitors will find a large population of black gooney birds, tropic birds, petrels, shearwaters, boobies, frigates and several

Laysan albatross near the old cable house, Sand Island, Midway.

others. Many of these birds are accustomed to humans, which allows you to easily observe and photograph them.

Midway is an excellent spot to encounter endemic **Hawaiian monk seals**. Once hunted for fur, meat and oil, these native Hawaiian mammals are now unfortunately endangered. On Midway they can often be seen basking on the beaches, some of which are closed to visitors to protect the seals. All Hawaiian monk seals are protected under both the Marine Mammal Protection Act and Endangered Species Act, and may not be disturbed in any way.

Hawaiian Monk Seals

Hawaiian monk seals (*Monachus schauinslandi*) are found on the sandy beaches and surrounding waters of Midway and other islands of the Northwestern Hawaiian archipelago. Females can reach a length of 7.5ft (2.3m) and weigh up to 600lbs (273kg). Males are a little smaller, reaching 6.8ft (2.1m) and weighing more than 500lbs (230kg). Adults have a silver-gray back fading to a cream-colored belly, though both back and belly darken with age.

Throughout the 19th century, Hawaiian monk seals were easily exploited by hunters. They are now listed as endangered and protected under the U.S. Endangered Species Act. The current population of 1,300 to 1,400 animals is still at risk, threatened by ingestion of harmful substances, decrease in food availability, intentional kills and incidental capture. Natural factors such as an inherently slow reproductive rate have made it difficult for the population to stabilize and re-establish itself. The protection of critical habitat and mitigation of human disturbance are critical conservation and protection strategies.

Diving Health & Safety

General Health

There are few serious health issues to be concerned with in Hawaii. Luckily, Hawaii is free of tropical diseases such as malaria, yellow fever and cholera. No immunizations are required to enter Hawaii or any other state in the U.S.

Generally, Hawaii provides some of the world's safest diving conditions, but when it's surgy the sharp, unforgiving lava rocks present a potential hazard to divers. Always stay alert for changing conditions whether you are entering the water or already underwater. The most notable health risks for Hawaii's visitors are sun overexposure, dehydration and heat exhaustion. These can all be easily prevented by using sunblock and protective clothing, choosing dive boats that provide a shaded area, drinking plenty of fluids, and slowing yourself down to "Hawaiian Time."

Pre-Trip Preparation

Your general state of health, diving skill level and specific equipment needs are the three most important factors that impact any dive trip. If you honestly assess these before you leave, you'll be well on your way to assuring a safe dive trip.

First, if you're not in shape, start exercising. Second, if you haven't dived for a while (six months is too long) and your skills are rusty, do a local dive with an experienced buddy or take a scuba review course. Finally, inspect your dive gear. Feeling good physically, diving with experience and with reliable equipment will not only increase your safety, but will also enhance your enjoyment underwater.

At least a month before your trip, inspect your dive gear. Remember, your regulator should be serviced annually, whether you've used it or not. If you use a dive computer and can replace the battery yourself, change it before the trip or buy a spare one to take along. Otherwise, send the computer to the manufacturer for a battery replacement.

If possible, find out if the dive center rents or services the

Diving & Flying

Most divers in Hawaii arrive by plane. While it's fine to dive soon *after* flying, it's important to remember that your last dive should be completed at least 12 hours (some experts advise 24 hours, particularly after repetitive dives) *before* your flight to minimize the risk of decompression sickness, caused by residual nitrogen in the blood.

type of gear you own. If not, you might want to take spare parts or even spare gear. A spare mask is always a good idea.

Purchase any additional equipment you might need, such as a dive light and tank marker light for night diving, a line reel for wreck diving, etc. Make sure you have at least a whistle attached to your BC. Better yet, add a marker tube (also known as a safety sausage or come-to-me).

About a week before taking off, do a final check of your gear, grease o-rings, check batteries and assemble a save-a-dive kit. This kit should at minimum contain extra mask and fin straps, snorkel keeper, mouthpiece, valve cap, zip ties and o-rings. Don't forget to pack a first-aid kit and medications such as decongestants, ear drops, antihistamines and seasickness tablets.

Signaling Devices

Occasionally a diver becomes lost or is left behind at a dive site—make sure this never happens to you! A diver is extremely difficult to locate in the water, so always dive with a signaling device of some sort, preferably more than one.

One of the best signaling devices and the easiest to carry is a whistle. Even the little ones are extremely effective. Use a zip tie to attach one permanently to your BC. Even better, though more expensive, is a loud airhorn that connects to the inflator hose. You simply push a button to let out a blast. It does require air from your tank to function, though.

In order to be seen as well as heard, you should also carry a marker tube. The best ones are bright in color and about 10ft (3m) high. They roll up and can easily fit into a BC pocket or be clipped onto a D ring. They're inflated orally or with a regulator. Some allow you to insert a dive light into the tube—a nice feature when it's dark.

Other signaling aides include mirrors, flares and dye markers, but these have limited reliability. A simple dive light is particularly versatile. Not only can it be used during the day for looking into crevices and crannies, it also comes in handy for nighttime signaling. Some even have a special strobe feature. Whenever you're diving, consider carrying at least a small light—you might encounter an unexpected night dive and be happy to have it.

DAN

Divers Alert Network (DAN) is an international membership association of individuals and organizations sharing a common interest in diving and safety. It operates a 24-hour diving emergency hot line in the U.S.: ☎ **919-684-8111 or 919-684-4DAN** (-4326). The latter accepts collect calls in a dive emergency. Though DAN does not directly provide medical care, it does provide advice on early treatment, evacuation and hyperbaric treatment of diving-related injuries. Divers should contact DAN for assistance as soon as a diving emergency is suspected.

DAN membership is reasonably priced and includes DAN TravelAssist, a membership benefit that covers medical air evacuation from anywhere in the world for any illness or injury. For a small additional fee, divers can get secondary insurance coverage for decompression sickness. For membership questions, contact DAN at ☎ 800-446-2671 from within the U.S. or ☎ 919-684-2948 from elsewhere. DAN can also be reached at www.diversalertnetwork.org.

Recompression & Medical Facilities

Hawaii has two recompression facilities equipped to treat dive-related decompression injuries, both on Oahu. In a dive emergency call 911, the Coast Guard or DAN. Each of these contacts can assess the situation and arrange for appropriate transportation to the nearest suitable facility. In such an emergency, don't contact or drive to a medical facility directly, as it may not be able to treat your condition.

Hawaii has 25 acute-care hospitals. While the rural islands of Molokai and Lanai have limited medical facilities, the other main islands have fully staffed hospitals with modern facilities. Midway visitors have access to a basic local medical facility staffed by a full-time licensed physician. The nearest complete medical and recompression facilities are on Oahu. Call ☎ 911 from any island to contact the nearest emergency facility.

Medical Contacts

All Emergencies:

| U.S. Emergency Operator | ☎ 911 |

Dive-Related Emergencies:

| U.S. Coast Guard Rescue Coordination Center | ☎ 541-2500 |
| Divers Alert Network (DAN) | ☎ 919-684-4326 |

General Medical Care:

Oahu	Queen's Medical Center	☎ 538-9011
Big Island	Kona Hospital	☎ 322-9311
	Hilo Hospital	☎ 974-4700
Maui	Maui Memorial Hospital	☎ 244-9056
Lanai	Lanai Community Hospital	☎ 565-6411
Kauai	Wilcox Memorial Hospital	☎ 245-1100

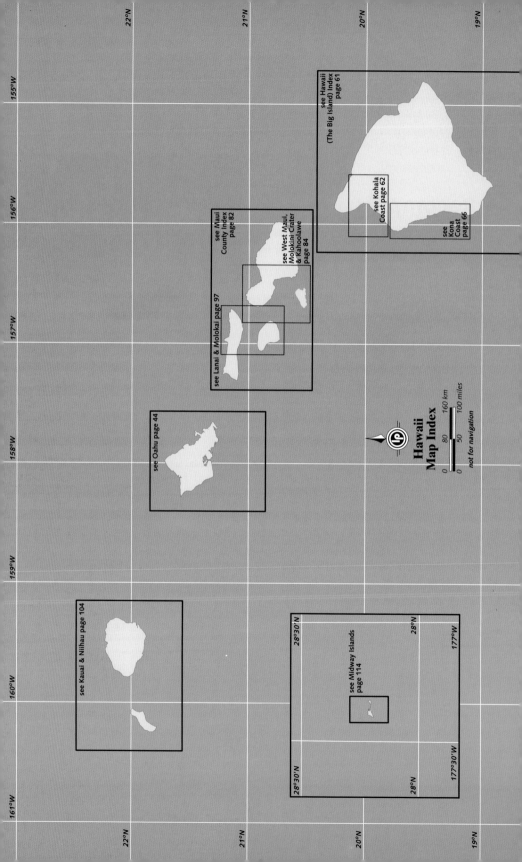

Hawaii
Map Index

see Kauai & Niihau page 104

see Oahu page 44

see Maui County Index page 82

see West Maui, Molokini Crater & Kahoolawe page 84

see Lanai & Molokai page 97

see Hawaii (The Big Island) Index page 61

see Kohala Coast page 62

see Kona Coast page 66

see Midway Islands page 114

0   80   160 km
0   50   100 miles
not for navigation

22°N
21°N
20°N
19°N

155°W
156°W
157°W
158°W
159°W
160°W
161°W

28°30'N
28°N
177°W
177°30'W

Diving
in Hawaii

With easy access to dive sites and favorable year-round water conditions, Hawaii has long been a popular scuba and snorkeling destination for visitors from around the world. Divers can look forward to spectacular lava caves, arches and other lava formations, along with a variety of wrecks and pristine hard-coral gardens. Divers can often enjoy watching dolphins play in a boat's wake. You may even see a humpback whale breach at the horizon during a boat ride to a dive site or at surface intervals. Some dive boat captains like to trawl for game fish between dives, and others may take you to a shallow spot so you can continue to enjoy the reefs while snorkeling as you off-gas.

Many diving and snorkeling sites are located directly offshore but, due to many factors, are only safely accessible by boat. Boat diving allows you to see the best the islands have to offer while providing a safer, more relaxing and fun experience. Dive boats vary in size and capacity: some boats take up to 6, others 12 and in some cases 24 or more passengers. Generally, dive operators will provide enough divemasters to divide divers into groups of six or less. Some operators cater to specific nationalities of divers (evident by brochures and advertising in many languages), though most are multicultural.

Volcano Diving

The unique underwater terrain formed by volcanic activity adds interest to nearly all of Hawaii's dive sites. Lava ridges and fingers often lay the base for coral reefs, while lava caves, caverns, tunnels and archways are spectacular to explore. Lava tends to be porous and covered with small nooks and crannies (called *pukas* in Hawaiian) that underwater critters convert into homes. Areas of relatively young lava activity—huge flows of coal-black lava where coral has not yet established itself—are dramatic seascapes in their own right.

Lava continues to flow into the sea every day from the still-active Kilauea Volcano on the Big Island. Many divers inquire about diving where the red-hot lava meets the ocean. Although technically possible, it is not recommended. Diving in the vicinity of volcanic activity is very dangerous. The water temperature is extremely hot and burns are almost inevitable. Underwater explosions and lava avalanches are quite common when the glowing lava and the cool salt water mix, and constitute additional dangers that divers are better off avoiding.

There are only two live-aboard vessels dedicated to scuba diving in Hawaii. Both operate along the Kona and Kohala Coasts of the Big Island. The *Kona Aggressor II* accommodates up to 10 passengers and is based out of Kailua-Kona. Charters generally run for a week. The *Sunseeker* operates out of Kawaihae Harbor on the Kohala Coast and caters to a maximum of six divers. Charter length and schedules vary based on divers' requests. See the "Listings" section for details.

In general, each island has only a few diving and snorkeling spots that can be safely enjoyed as shore dives. Shore diving accessibility is affected by Hawaii's unpredictable and quickly changing weather patterns. A local dive guide can help you select the safest shore dives given the current weather conditions. If you are on a tight budget, you may want to dive the popular shore diving areas on the weekends, where you can watch local divers enter the water (often a tricky task on Hawaii's rocky coastlines) and perhaps ask a few questions. Be sure to stop by a local dive shop for professional advice and guidance. Some dive operators organize local shore dives that are guided by a professional divemaster. This combines safety with specific information about each site's unique highlights at a price that generally suits even budget-oriented divers.

Hawaii's active local diving community takes part in a variety of dive clubs, underwater photography competitions and underwater cleanup efforts, and has formed a coalition (the Lost Coast Coalition) to protect the island chain's precious reef fish from over-collection by tropical fish collectors. Visiting divers can usually participate in local activities if their timing is good. Ask about current activities at the local dive shops when you arrive.

Dive Training & Certification

If you have never dived before, Hawaii is the perfect place to start. The clear tropical water and colorful shallow reefs are forgiving for first-time divers. Recent changes to entry-level diving requirements have made learning to dive easier than ever before, without compromising safety. Just about anyone in reasonably good health can venture underwater here and breathe air. Whether you want to try diving for the first time or are looking for advanced certification, you are likely to find a program that meets your needs and goals.

Some organizations offer pool-only scuba programs for children 8 to 11 years old. For people aged 12 and up, beginner programs such as the popular "resort course" start you out in either a pool or a calm, shallow ocean site. Upon successful completion of this confined water session, you will be qualified to dive with a professional instructor for the duration of your holiday. The dives and any of the

An instructor demonstrates how to use the equipment.

Snuba Diving

Designed as an introduction to diving, snuba is a hybrid of diving and snorkeling. Snuba divers breathe compressed air like a scuba diver, but the air is supplied via a regulator and 20 to 40ft- (6 to 12m-) long hose connected to an air tank. The tank floats in a raft on the surface of the water. A small harness keeps the regulator in place.

Without the heavy and technical equipment normally associated with diving, snuba is far less intimidating than a "real" dive. Snuba makes underwater exploration easier than either snorkeling or free-diving since you don't have to hold your breath or constantly return to the surface for air. Even kids eight years and older can do this with only a little training, and a lot of success. There are a few disadvantages: snuba depths are limited by the length of the hose, and snuba diving can't be safely performed in areas with lava formations, currents, wrecks or anywhere else where the hoses could get tangled.

Snuba is a fun and easy way to explore Hawaii's reefs.

accomplished skills may be credited toward your Open Water certification (as long as you complete certification within 12 months). The specifics of these programs can vary, so inquire before you sign up.

Full certification classes are available for those with varying budgets and time constraints. If you have only a few days, you may need to sign up for a one-on-one class with an instructor who can modify the course to fit your schedule. Generally a minimum of four days is needed.

If time is not an issue but you have a limited budget, you can join a class designed for residents. These classes are generally held in the evening or on weekends over the course of a few weeks or months. The cost may be as low as $100, but varies with the number of students enrolled and if materials or boat dives are included.

There are many options that fall between the more expensive but fast private lessons and the inexpensive but lengthy group classes. Options vary between dive operators and prices often hinge on the number of students in the class.

Another popular option is the Open Water referral program. You complete the pool and classroom sessions at a dive shop near home, then conduct the open water or check-out dives while vacationing in Hawaii. There are some restrictions and time limits, so be sure to get specific information from both your local dive shop and the Hawaiian operator well ahead of time.

If you are already a certified diver, you'll find that many of the dive shops throughout the main islands offer a wide range of specialty classes, including various technical diving courses. Call ahead for class schedules and requirements for the courses you're interested in.

Snorkeling

Many of Hawaii's dive sites—particularly the shallow, sheltered bays—are just as rewarding and enjoyable for snorkelers as they are for divers. Snorkeling is certainly the easiest and generally the least expensive way to enjoy the underwater world. You only need a mask, snorkel and fins, though additional items may be desirable. Flotation devices such as an inflatable vest, an inner tube or a kickboard can enhance the experience. A long-sleeved T-shirt or lycra skin will help prevent sunburn, and rubber-soled booties are essential in areas that involve walking over sharp lava rocks to reach the snorkeling entry location.

If you plan to snorkel from shore, it is advisable to hire a local guide or stay in areas that are under the supervision of a lifeguard. Be sure to inquire about prevailing currents and other possible hazards, then evaluate your physical abilities against the conditions. Shore entry and snorkeling near shore can be complicated by the waves and currents—never turn your back to the ocean.

Hawaii's Top 10 Snorkeling Spots

4	Magic Island (Oahu)
8	Inside Reef (Oahu)
14	Three Tables (Oahu)
21	Kaiwi Point (Big Island)
23	Kahaluu (Big Island)
28	Kealakekua Bay (Big Island)
29	Place of Refuge (Big Island)
34	Black Rock (Maui)
38	Inside Crater (Maui)
55	Kee Lagoon (Kauai)

You'll have up-close and personal encounters with fish while snorkeling in Hawaii's shallow bays.

Waves can take you by surprise if you are not alert. They generally come in sets, so if one passes, another is likely to be close behind.

Joining a boat cruise is usually the safest snorkeling option. On all major islands you'll find many businesses offer half-day snorkel tours that generally include snorkeling instruction, equipment, additional flotation devices, freshwater showers, snacks and/or lunch. This is a great way to spend half a day.

Pisces Rating System for Dives & Divers

The dive sites in this book are rated according to the following diver skill-level rating system. These are not absolute ratings but apply to divers at a particular time, diving at a particular place. For instance, someone unfamiliar with prevailing conditions might be considered a novice diver at one dive area, but an intermediate diver at another, more familiar location.

Novice: A novice diver should be accompanied by an instructor, divemaster or advanced diver on all dives. A novice diver generally fits the following profile:
◆ basic scuba certification from an internationally recognized certifying agency
◆ dives infrequently (less than one trip a year)
◆ logged fewer than 25 total dives
◆ little or no experience diving in similar waters and conditions
◆ dives no deeper than 60ft (18m)

Intermediate: An intermediate diver generally fits the following profile:
◆ may have participated in some form of continuing diver education
◆ logged between 25 and 100 dives
◆ dives no deeper than 130ft (40m)
◆ has been diving in similar waters and conditions within the last six months

Advanced: An advanced diver generally fits the following profile:
◆ advanced certification
◆ has been diving for more than two years and logged over 100 dives
◆ has been diving in similar waters and conditions within the last six months

Regardless of your skill level, you should be in good physical condition and know your limitations. If you are uncertain of your own level of expertise for a particular site, ask the advice of a local dive instructor. He or she is best qualified to assess your abilities based on the site's prevailing dive conditions. Ultimately, however, you must decide if you are capable of making a particular dive, a decision that should take into account your level of training, recent experience and physical condition, as well as the conditions at the site. Remember that conditions can change at any time, even during a dive.

Dive Site Icons

The symbols at the beginning of each dive site description provide a quick summary of some of the important characteristics of each site:

 Good snorkeling or free-diving site.

 Remains or partial remains of a wreck can be seen at this site.

 Sheer wall or drop-off.

 Deep dive. Features of this dive are found in water deeper than 90ft (27m).

 Strong currents may be encountered at this site.

 Strong surge (the horizontal movement of water caused by waves) may be encountered at this site.

 Drift dive. Because of strong currents and/or difficulty in anchoring, a drift dive is recommended at this site.

 Shore dive. This site can be accessed from shore.

 Poor visibility. The site often has visibility of less than 25ft (8m).

 Caves or caverns are a prominent feature of this site. Only experienced cave divers should explore inner cave areas.

 Marine preserve. Special protective regulations apply in this area.

Oahu Dive Sites

Oahu is by far the most developed of the islands, with a culturally and ethnically diverse population of close to a million people. This melting pot of peoples and cultures offers all the excitement of a large cosmopolitan area alongside the pleasures of a tropical island: nightlife, fine dining and interesting museums complement great beaches, surfing and good diving and snorkeling.

Oahu is the only island in Hawaii that offers several first-class wreck dives, which continue to get better as their marine life populations become more dense. Several shallow reefs make excellent shore dives for both divers and snorkelers. Although Oahu's reefs do not generally have the pristine coral and superb visibility found on most of the other islands, there is a nice balance of reef dives and volcanic cavern dives with swirling, colorful fish.

Diver discovers a pincushion sea star on the reef at Oahu's Makaha Caverns.

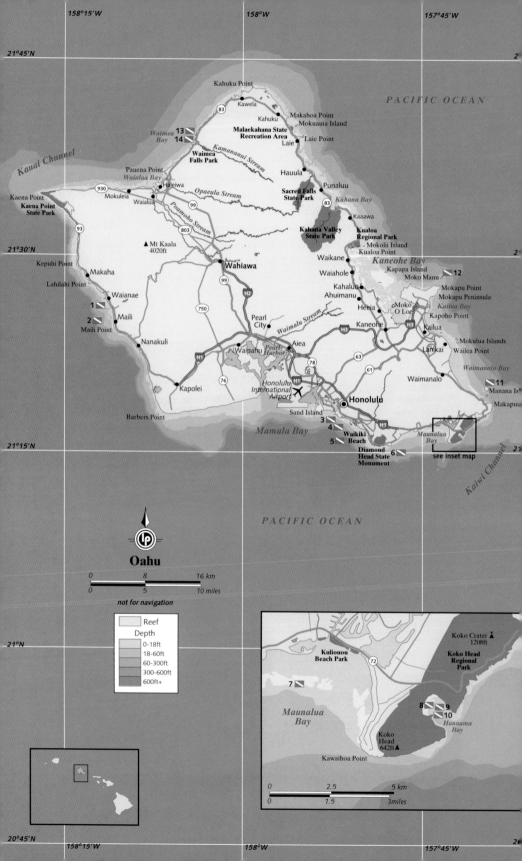

Oahu

Legend

Reef

Depth
- 0-18ft
- 18-60ft
- 60-300ft
- 300-600ft
- 600ft+

not for navigation

0 8 16 km
0 5 10 miles

PACIFIC OCEAN

158°15'W · 158°W · 157°45'W

21°45'N
21°30'N
21°N
20°45'N

Kahuku Point
Kawela
Kahuku
Makahoa Point
Mokuauia Island
Laie Point
Malaekahana State Recreation Area
Laie
Waimea Bay 13 14
Waimea Falls Park
Pauena Point
Waialua Bay
Haleiwa
Mokuleia
Waialua
Opaeula Stream
Hauula
Sacred Falls State Park
Punaluu
Kahana Bay
Kahana Valley State Park
Kaaawa
Kualoa Regional Park
Mokolii Island
Kualoa Point

Kauai Channel
Kaena Point
Kaena Point State Park
93
930
803
99
Poamoho Stream
Kamananui Stream
▲ Mt Kaala 4020ft
Wahiawa
99
H2
Waimalu Stream
Waikane
Waiahole
Kahaluu
Ahuimanu
Heeia
Kaneohe
Kaneohe Bay
Kapapa Island
Moko Manu 12
Moko O Loe
Mokapu Point
Mokapu Peninsula
Kailua Bay
Kapoho Point
Kailua
Lanikai
Mokulua Islands
Wailea Point

Kepuhi Point
Makaha
Lahilahi Point
Waianae
Maili
1
2
Maili Point
Nanakuli
Kapolei
Barbers Point
750
H1
76
Pearl City
Waipahu
Pearl Harbor
Aiea
Honolulu International Airport
78
H1
H1
63
61
H3
H3
Waimanalo
Waimanalo Bay
11
Manana Is
Makapuu
Honolulu
3
4
Waikiki Beach
5
6
Diamond Head State Monument
Maunalua Bay
see inset map
Mamala Bay

PACIFIC OCEAN
Kaiwi Channel

Inset map

Koko Crater ▲ 1208ft
Koko Head Regional Park
Kuliouou Beach Park
72
7
Maunalua Bay
8 9 10
Koko Head 642ft ▲
Hanauma Bay
Kawaihoa Point

0 2.5 5 km
0 1.5 3 miles

As the most populated and most visited Hawaiian island, Oahu has the greatest number of dive operators and dive shops, the majority of which are modern and up-to-date. Equipment rentals and airfills are easily available around the island. Many of Oahu's local residents are divers. You will find that some of the shops specialize in teaching courses designed for locals, while others cater mostly to visitors.

Dive sites on Oahu are divided into four main regions: the leeward side, the south coast (including Hanauma Bay), the windward side and the north shore.

Oahu Dive Sites	Good Snorkeling	Novice	Intermediate	Advanced
1 Makaha Caverns	●		●	
2 The *Mahi*			●	
3 Koala Pipe		●		
4 Magic Island	●	●		
5 *YO-257*			●	
6 Corsair				●
7 Turtle Canyon	●	●		
8 Inside Reef	●	●		
9 Outside Reef	●		●	
10 Witch's Brew				●
11 Manana Island				●
12 Moku Manu				●
13 Shark's Cove	●		●	
14 Three Tables	●		●	

Leeward Side

Oahu's sheltered leeward side, extending from Kaena Point to Diamond Head, is one of the state's most popular diving areas because of its nearly year-round accessibility. There are several wrecks that shelter a variety of fish and coral species from the strong currents that often flow through the area. Lava formations provide additional places to look for interesting marine life.

1 Makaha Caverns

Makaha Caverns is an interesting shallow site that can be spectacular when the visibility is good. Normal visibility is 50 to 60ft, though it can be as much as 100ft when the seas are calm and there has been little rain or runoff to cloud the water.

There are two large open-ended lava tubes that form a V-shaped cavern found about a hundred yards from shore. Near the openings you can expect to see large schools of bluestripe snappers and yellowstripe goatfish. The tubes are easy to swim through. With the help of a flashlight, you'll discover several dense schools of soldierfish, along with Hawaiian bigeyes and squirrelfish.

The large rubble area that surrounds the cavern is worth checking for octopuses, devil scorpionfish and juvenile dragon wrasses. With just a little bit of luck, you may even see mantas and green sea turtles in the vicinity.

If you like to combine night diving with the comfort of boat diving, then

Location: West of Waianae Boat Harbor

Depth Range: 20-45ft (6-14m)

Access: Boat or shore

Expertise Rating: Intermediate

this is your spot. It's shallow, easy diving with very little current (though occasionally it can be surgy) and has an abundance of nocturnal life. All the critters that hide inside during the daytime—such as reef crabs, spiny lobsters, colorful reef shrimp and Spanish dancers—come out onto the open reef to feed. It is not recommended to enter the cavern at night, even when conditions are calm. First, it may be disorienting since it's too dark to clearly see the exit, and second, the critters are all out on the reef.

The camouflage of the venomous devil scorpionfish allows it to blend into the rubble. Its eyes are the only things that distinguish it from the rocky background.

Building the Perfect Reef

The best way for divers to understand reef evolution is to observe artificial reefs that are at different stages of development. Artificial reefs can be made of any foreign object that has been submerged: ship or plane wrecks, "junk" like tires or bottles, and concrete blocks. Even broken-up wrecks with their parts scattered about lend themselves well to marine life encrustation and are generally worth at least a couple of dives. The more you look, the more you'll see.

The abundance of marine life and coral growth on an artificial reef depends on three main factors:

Location: Reefs (both natural and artificial) provide animals with shelter from the current and predators. Artificial reefs placed in open, sandy areas become oases for the surrounding marine life. Hence, this type of reef tends to feature a denser concentration of marine life than an area on an open coral reef, where there are many more places to find shelter. The *Mahi* and the *YO-257* wrecks, which were both purposely sunk in large sandy areas, are good examples of this principle.

The shelter that artificial reefs provide in current-swept locations often attracts species that are otherwise rarely seen. Juveniles also commonly take refuge. Hydroids and sponges draw an abundant nudibranch population.

Material: Steel generally provides an easy surface for coral to grow on. Rubber and aluminum objects, though they may provide excellent shelter, are more difficult for coral to grow on.

Age: Generally, coral takes at least a few years to establish itself. Other species are gradually attracted as the coral becomes more profuse. The longer the object has been underwater, the more populated and interesting the artificial reef becomes.

Large schools of bluestripe snapper seek shelter near The *Mahi* wreck.

2   The *Mahi*

This is truly a terrific dive with lots to see and explore. The 165ft-long ship was originally built for the U.S. Navy, was later converted into an oceanographic research ship and then was purposely sunk in 1982 as an artificial reef. Since then the wreck has become Oahu's most popular and exciting dive.

Location: Southwest of Waianae Boat Harbor

Depth Range: 60-95ft (18-29m)

Access: Boat

Expertise Rating: Intermediate

The ship can be entered when water conditions allow, but only advanced divers should consider penetration. If you plan to enter the wreck, be sure to take a good dive light along. Inside you may encounter soldierfish, squirrelfish, spiny lobsters and crabs.

It is the outside of the wreck where most of the marine life is found. Over the

Wreck Diving

Wreck diving can be safe and fascinating. Penetration of shipwrecks, however, is a skilled specialty and should not be attempted without proper training. Wrecks are often unstable; they can be silty, deep and disorienting. Use an experienced guide to view wrecks and the amazing coral communities that have developed on them.

years an abundance of sponges and corals have established themselves on the wreck. Lovely snowflake and tubastrea (cup) corals decorate the portholes and ceilings, while orange, yellow and red sponges encrust the walls, making for terrific photo opportunities. Large schools of lemon butterflyfish and bluestripe snappers swarm approaching divers, while huge porcupine pufferfish hover just above the wreck. Keep your eyes peeled for the resident school of eagle rays and the rare Hawaiian stingrays that cruise the sandy area surrounding The *Mahi*.

Toward the ship's stern you can usually find several yellowmargin morays. Some of them have been fed by divemasters and tend to be quite friendly. Be respectful of them: don't touch them.

Look for The *Mahi's* resident school of eagle rays cruising the sandy areas near the wreck.

3 Koala Pipe

This may not be the most dramatic site in Oahu, but it is a convenient, shallow dive that can be very enjoyable if you know what to look for. The underwater steel pipeline is now broken into pieces, making an artificial reef that offers shelter to a variety of fish species. Near the pipe look for devil scorpionfish, leaf fish and the endemic titan scorpionfish. These venomous (but slow moving) creatures are great photo subjects.

Surrounding the pipe at a depth of 30 to 40ft you will find a coral reef consisting of several small ridges. You'll find a great variety of juvenile fish within the protection of the finger coral, along with Potter's angelfish and some of the less common and endemic wrasses. The beautiful pearl wrasse, belted wrasse and shortnose wrasse are among the more intriguing endemic species.

In the rubble patches between the reef structures you may encounter the small dragon wrasse, which resembles a piece of seaweed dancing over the rocks in the surge, or you might see the reptilian bottom-dwelling lizardfish. Koala Pipe is also an excellent site for spotting some of the Hawaiian Islands' most colorful nudibranchs and octopuses.

Location: West of Honolulu

Depth: 40ft (12m)

Access: Boat

Expertise Rating: Novice

A diver emerges from one of the coral-encrusted pipes at Koala Pipe.

4 Magic Island

This dive site is known as both Magic Island and Rainbow Reef. Its popularity is mostly due to its convenient location near Ala Moana Beach Park (north of Waikiki) and its easy shore access to the inside of the cove. Divers and snorkelers need to be aware of possible boat traffic in this area.

The first 100 yards from shore are shallow and offer only limited visibility, but the abundance of "tame" hand-fed fish makes up for it. Here you'll be able to get quite close to a variety of fish that are normally skittish and hard to approach.

Location: West of Honolulu

Depth Range: 30-50ft (9-15m)

Access: Shore

Expertise Rating: Novice

Another attraction for experienced fish-watchers is the juveniles and rare species found in this area. The sheltered lagoon is an ideal home for many fish that are not normally found on open reefs. The area is also excellent for finding unusual and colorful nudibranchs.

Once you get out of the cove, the depth drops to about 50ft and water clarity improves. The terrain consists mostly of sand and coral formations with some cave formations in the channels that connect the cove with the open water. With some luck you may encounter manta rays or sea turtles on this dive.

BEVERLY FACTOR

Magic Island is a great site to find colorful nudibranchs.

5 YO-257

This is a unique dive site in many ways. The former navy oiler was purposely sunk by Atlantis Submarine International, Inc. to serve as an artificial reef and an attraction for their submarine-tour passengers. The 110ft-long vessel has rested upright in near-perfect condition on the sandy seafloor just off the shore of Waikiki since 1989.

Location: West of Waikiki

Depth Range: 55-100ft (17-30m)

Access: Boat

Expertise Rating: Intermediate

During your dive on the YO-257 you are likely to see an Atlantis submarine glide by.

During your dive you are likely to see an Atlantis submarine gliding by with all the passengers waving at you and taking snapshots from their dry environment. This is quite an unusual encounter and makes for an interesting dive. Be careful not to approach the submarine too closely, since its thrusters generate quite a bit of turbulence.

Although the submarine experience is fun, there is

more to see at this site. Because of the wreck's position on the sandy bottom, it is like an oasis in an underwater desert. Huge schools of friendly lemon butterflyfish, goatfish and bluestripe snappers swim around this marine life magnet. The variety of nudibranchs near the sponges and hydroids is among the best you'll find anywhere in Hawaii. Expect to see green sea turtles, yellowmargin and whitemouth morays, porcupine pufferfish, boxfish, broomtail filefish and much more. If you're an inquisitive diver with a keen eye, you may find one of the well-camouflaged giant frogfish that live on the wreck.

Wide-angle photographers will be pleased to find a variety of great photo opportunities, including images of *YO-257*'s portholes, which are beautifully decorated with snowflake-like hydroids. Some of the portholes are accessible from the interior.

If you plan to photograph your buddy peeking through one, warn him or her ahead of time that the hydroids have a nasty sting.

Be careful not to touch the hydroids as you approach the *YO-257*'s portholes.

6 Corsair

The Corsair is the only wreck visited by divers in Oahu that was not intentionally sunk as an artificial reef. While on a training mission off the coast of Hawaii Kai in 1946, the pilot ran out of fuel and safely bailed out before the plane plunged into the water southeast of Diamond Head.

The plane, which was left to rest on the sandy bottom, has become an oasis in an otherwise barren, current-swept seascape. Now embellished by colorful sponges and several coral structures, the Corsair shelters an interesting selection of fish species. Eagle rays and green sea

Location: Southeast of Diamond Head

Depth: 107ft (32m)

Access: Boat

Expertise Rating: Advanced

turtles are among the larger residents that frequent the wreck. Due to its depth and the amount there is to see, this is a good site for nitrox-certified divers to extend their bottom time.

South Coast/Hanauma Bay

Along the south coast, which extends from Diamond Head to Makapuu Point, you will find a panoramic coastline that is characterized by sheer cliffs and often-times pounding surf. This area also feels the grip of a treacherous current known as the "Molokai Express," produced by the prevailing northeast trade winds. This water movement is weakest near shore, so stay close when diving here.

Hanauma Bay, Hawaii's most scenic snorkeling spot if you don't mind the crowds, is located along the south coast. The bay, a marine life conservation district since 1967, attracts up to 10,000 visitors each day.

Part of the cone of this former volcano has collapsed into the ocean, forming a picture-perfect sandy cove that is protected from the elements. The water is calm almost every day of the year, making it the perfect spot for first-time snorkelers.

Though Hanauma Bay has several sites that are interesting and appropriate for divers, not all sites are safely accessible from shore. Be sure to assess the weather and surf conditions and your physical ability before starting out.

Hanauma Bay from above.

7 Turtle Canyon

The best place to spot green sea turtles on Oahu is at this dive site, just off the island's south coast. You are almost guaranteed to see at least a few of them as you descend to the shallow reef, which has an average depth of only about 30ft. You are most likely to find them resting on the rubble-covered sandy bottom or on the coral reef itself. Since they are accustomed to divers, they will usually allow you to get close, but please do not touch them!

As you would expect, this is a prime location to photograph these protected

Location: Maunalua Bay

Depth Range: 30-40ft (9-12m)

Access: Boat

Expertise Rating: Novice

marine reptiles. A camera system with a 20mm or 28mm lens is ideal, but since the dive is so shallow and the light conditions are good, you can get a decent shot even with a disposable underwater camera.

In addition to the resident turtle population, you can expect to see large schools of durgeonfish (which tend to swarm divers), along with soldierfish and hermit crabs, shrimp, nudibranchs and other little creatures that live underneath the numerous overhangs and ledges. Be sure not to ignore the rubble patches, since they are home to interesting small animals, too.

Both snorkelers and divers can enjoy close encounters with green sea turtles at Turtle Canyon.

Sea Turtle Conservation

Throughout the world there are eight species of sea turtles. Green sea turtles are the most common species seen in Hawaii's tropical waters. They can grow up to 4ft (1.2m) long and weigh up to 300lbs (135kg). Hawksbill turtles—which reach up to 3ft (1m) in length and weigh as much as 165lbs (74kg)—also inhabit the region, though they are seldom seen by divers on the reefs. Both species are endangered and protected by law: do not touch or molest sea turtles in any way.

Dangers contributing to the demise of these creatures include: hunting for human consumption, turtle-shell jewelry and ornaments; loss of habitat due to tourism and development; pollution; getting trapped in fishing nets; and injury from ship propellers and boat traffic.

What can you do to help turtles survive?

✓ Don't disturb or frighten a sea turtle, especially during mating season (June through August).

✓ Don't eat turtle eggs, turtle soup or any other turtle dish.

✓ Don't buy or use any product made from turtle shell.

✓ Encourage efforts to preserve turtle-nesting beaches as natural reserves.

8 Inside Reef

This is the most protected and shallowest area of Hanauma Bay and is more suitable for snorkeling than diving. Due to the large crowds, the coral is not in very good shape anymore. The thousands of snorkelers and swimmers kick up sand, which clouds up the water as the day progresses. The practice of feeding the fish with bread also contributes to the poor visibility. For better visibility and less-crowded conditions, it is best to dive or snorkel here is as early as possible: the park opens at 6am.

This is a perfect area for underwater photographers seeking to get good,

Location: Hanauma Bay

Depth Range: 5-20ft (2-6m)

Access: Shore

Expertise Rating: Novice

close-up fish shots. The wide variety of butterflyfish are so tame that they'll swim right up to your lens, and the shallow depth allows divers to stay underwater for a long time.

Both adult and juvenile Picasso and lagoon triggerfish can be seen here. Rainbow-hued parrotfish are common, along with an array of butterflyfish such as the endemic bluestripe butterflyfish, raccoon butterflyfish and the largest of all, the stunning lined butterflyfish. Underwater photographers will be pleased to find that fast-swimming, shallow-water wrasses such as surge, Christmas and fivestripe wrasses—which all boast brilliant color patterns—are relatively easy to approach.

Hawaii's state fish, the Picasso triggerfish, is found in the shallow water of Inside Reef.

9 Outside Reef

For more-experienced snorkelers and divers, Outside Reef can be very rewarding. Visibility tends to be much better than at Inside Reef, the coral is in better shape and marine life is plentiful. As long as you don't go too far out, you'll still be within the protection of the bay.

The mostly sandy bottom and the scattered coral heads are inhabited by bluestripe, raccoon and threadfin butterflyfish, arc-eye hawkfish, Christmas and surge wrasses, triggerfish and tangs.

Location: Hanauma Bay

Depth Range: 15-70ft (5-21m)

Access: Shore

Expertise Rating: Intermediate

To leave the inner reef and reach the Outside Reef, do not try to swim over the barrier reef. This can be extremely hazardous, since any amount of surge can wash you across the surface of the coral. There is a passage known as "the slot" that provides a convenient entry and exit point between the inner and outer reefs. The slot is located on the right (southwest) side of the bay, in front of the lifeguard stand. A large cable runs through the channel near the surface and is a convenient guide back to the inner reef.

It is easy to see how the arc-eye hawkfish got its name.

10 Witch's Brew

This is a particularly nice spot on the right (southwest) side of Hanauma Bay, found where a small peninsula juts out from shore. In front of the peninsula is a coral garden with a healthy marine life population.

Location: Hanauma Bay

Depth Range: 40-50ft (12-15m)

Access: Shore

Expertise Rating: Advanced

This area got its name from the seething cauldron of multiple wave and current patterns that merge at this point, and from the area's wicked surge. Although the often-turbulent waters are the reason for the abundant marine life, they can make for a challenging dive.

One way to get to the site is to walk along the right-hand side of the bay until you reach the small peninsula. This is, however, a long walk when carrying heavy scuba equipment, particularly if you are lugging underwater camera equipment as well.

The other option is to follow the slot in Hanuama Bay (see dive site 9, Outside Reef) through the barrier reef, then stay to the right and swim toward the peninsula. Either way, this site requires some "commuting," but it is worth it for more experienced and adventurous divers.

Schooling damsels and tangs are often found in the surge zone at Witch's Brew.

Windward Side

The shoreline between Makapuu Point and Kahuku Point on Oahu's windward side is only diveable during kona weather—for those few days when the trade winds are absent—which can occur occasionally throughout the year, but is more likely between November and April.

Oahu's windward side is normally characterized by large waves and choppy seas and can only be dived on the few days when trade winds are absent.

11   Manana Island

Manana Island is a seabird sanctuary just offshore from Sealife Park. Although this island appears to be close to shore, it is actually quite a distance and you should not attempt to dive this site from shore.

Divers need to be aware that this site is frequented by the torrential Molokai Express current and should plan their dive accordingly. Be sure to follow your guide's instructions. The Molokai

Location: Waimanalo Bay

Depth Range: 40-70ft (12-21m)

Access: Boat

Expertise Rating: Advanced

Express tends to bring clear water to this site, along with many large game fish such as trevally, tuna, billfish and sharks, including tiger sharks.

The best diving is found on the seaward side of Manana Island and along a ridge that connects the island with adjacent Kaohikaipu Island. There are many over-hangs along the ridge that are laden with lobsters and other crustaceans. Triton's trumpet shells, many species of beautiful cowries and other shelled snails are also commonly spotted along the ridge.

You'll find a variety of shelled snails, including the beautiful tiger cowrie.

12 Moku Manu

Location: North of Mokapu Point

Depth Range: 30-90ft (9-27m)

Access: Boat

Expertise Rating: Advanced

Moku Manu is a two-island remnant of the Koolau Volcano. Due to its location on the windward side of Oahu, this site is not dived frequently, and the rich environment and abundant marine life are unmarred by overuse. Large parrotfish, unicorn fish, tuna and trevally are commonly observed. There are several dive sites around the two rocky islands, but wind is generally the determining factor when choosing where to dive. Also be aware of the strong, swift current that often sweeps between the islands and Mokapu Point. Carefully assess the safety conditions of sites in this area before diving.

One of the most popular areas to dive is a large cave between the two islands. The inside of the cave is dark, so be sure to bring a light to see the lobsters, crimson squirrelfish and soldierfish that inhabit the area. Outside the cave, you will encounter lush coral growth and an abundance of tropical fish. Green sea turtles are also occasionally spotted at the nearby sandy channel.

The seaward side of the northern island features a skirting shelf at 30ft that first drops to 90ft, then plummets below recreational diving limits. Along the shelf you'll find numerous lava tubes and caves that are home to huge lobsters, yellowmargin morays and whitemouth morays. Sightings of tunas and other large fish are quite possible along the drop-off—just be sure to look toward the blue water to see what may swim by.

Masses of tropical fish, including this unicornfish, hang around the cave mouth at Moku Manu.

North Shore

Oahu's north shore, between Kahuku Point and Kaena Point, exhibits a ribbon of sandy beaches and numerous coves and bays. During the winter months huge swells make this region undiveable, but during the summer there are many good dive sites that are suitable for all levels.

Shark's Cove, like many north shore dive sites, can be undiveable during the winter due to wave action.

13 Shark's Cove

Named after a rock formation that very loosely resembles a shark (an imaginative diver must have come up with the name), this site is one of the most popular along Oahu's north shore. During the summer, when conditions tend to be calm, this is an excellent dive for novice divers and snorkelers due to the lack of current and wave action. This also makes it an ideal site for dive training, and instructors often conduct their classes here.

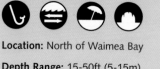

Location: North of Waimea Bay

Depth Range: 15-50ft (5-15m)

Access: Shore

Expertise Rating: Novice

Advanced divers are generally intrigued by the extensive tunnel and cave system that is found just outside the cove to the right. There is a lot to see at this site and the caverns are fun to explore, but be sure not to go beyond your level of training and comfort. If you are not familiar with the hazards of cave diving, it is recommended that you enter only if accompanied by a professional dive guide. With any surge present, exploration of the caverns can be disorienting and potentially hazardous. Even under calm conditions, sand and silt kicked up from divers' fins will cloud the water, making it easy to become disoriented.

This is also an excellent night dive, but unless you are an experienced diver who is already familiar with the site and the local weather conditions, you should not

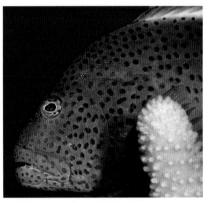
Blacksided or spotted hawkfish can be found in the coral gardens near Shark's Cove.

attempt night diving without a guide. During the winter months this site is inaccessible due to high surf conditions.

14 Three Tables

Less than one mile down the road from Shark's Cove is an outstanding shore dive for intermediate and advanced divers. Named after the three flat offshore lava rocks that break the surface of the water and then drop to 50ft, this site provides divers with spectacular seascapes includ-

Location: North of Waimea Bay

Depth Range: 15-50ft (5-15m)

Access: Shore

Expertise Rating: Intermediate

Large conger eels can be found occasionally at Three Tables.

ing arches, overhangs, tunnels and small caverns. The best diving is found to the right, reached by swimming diagonally in the direction of Shark's Cove. You can anticipate seeing a colorful medley of reef fish, lots of moray eels and even large conger eels.

If you swim farther out into deeper water you will also find a nice hard-coral reef inhabited by butterflyfish, Moorish idols and other colorful tropicals. Since Three Tables is located on the surf-prone north shore, you can safely access this site only during the summer months.

Big Island Dive Sites

The island of Hawaii is known as the Big Island, and rightly so—the Big Island comprises a land mass twice as large as all other Hawaiian Islands combined. In addition to some of the best diving conditions in the world, the Big Island is also graced with high, snow-capped mountain peaks and an active volcano. With relatively little development, the island has plenty of uncrowded places.

Diving around the Big Island varies greatly by region and is affected by weather and topography. High mountains protect most of the island's west coast from the northeast trade winds. Because of this, most dive sites are found along the sheltered, west-facing leeward Kohala and Kona Coasts. Though these coasts offer the best diving conditions on the island, most sites are difficult or unsafe to access from shore and require an understanding of the local conditions for safe diving.

The Big Island's windward Hilo side faces directly into the trade winds and is rarely diveable. If you want to explore the Hilo side, hire a professional and knowledgeable guide. There are a few dive shops in Hilo that cater mostly to locals and offer guided shore dives.

Diver explores a Kohala Coast cavern's beautiful red encrusting sponges.

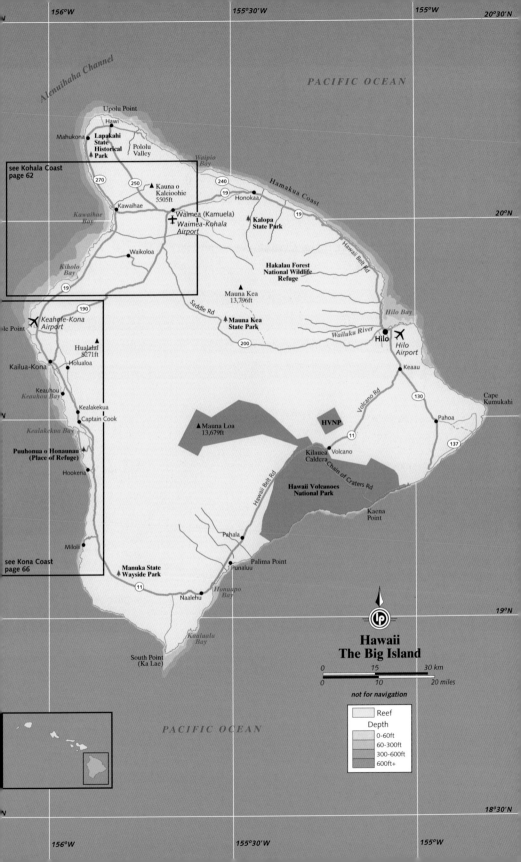

Hawaii
The Big Island

not for navigation

Reef
Depth
0-60ft
60-300ft
300-600ft
600ft+

see Kohala Coast
page 62

see Kona Coast
page 66

PACIFIC OCEAN

PACIFIC OCEAN

Alenuihaha Channel

Upolu Point

Hawi

Mahukona

Lapakahi State Historical Park

Pololu Valley

Waipio Bay

270

250

▲ Kauna o Kaleioohie 5505ft

240

19

Honokaa

Hamakua Coast

Kawaihae

Kawaihae Bay

Waimea (Kamuela)
Waimea-Kohala Airport

19

Kalopa State Park

Hawaii Belt Rd

Waikoloa

Kiholo Bay

19

Hakalau Forest National Wildlife Refuge

Mauna Kea 13,796ft ▲

Saddle Rd

Hilo Bay

190

Keahole-Kona Airport

le Point

▲ Hualalai 8271ft

Holualoa

Kailua-Kona

▲ **Mauna Kea State Park**

200

Wailuku River

Hilo

Hilo Airport

Keauhou
Keauhou Bay

Kealakekua

Captain Cook

Kealakekua Bay

Keaau

130

Cape Kumukahi

Pahoa

Volcano Rd

Puuhonua o Honaunau (Place of Refuge)

Hookena

▲ Mauna Loa 13,679ft

HVNP

11

Kilauea Caldera

Volcano

137

Chain of Craters Rd

Milolii

Hawaii Volcanoes National Park

Hawaii Belt Rd

Kaena Point

Manuka State Wayside Park

11

Pahala

Palima Point

Punaluu

Honuupo Bay

Naalehu

Kaalualu Bay

South Point (Ka Lae)

0   15   30 km
0   10   20 miles

Kohala Coast

The Kohala Coast lies along the northwest, leeward shore of the Big Island. It is more influenced by the trade winds than the Kona Coast to the south. As a result it is not always suitable for diving. However, when conditions are favorable, a number of dive sites are available. Many of them feature beautiful hard-coral gardens or fascinating lava formations.

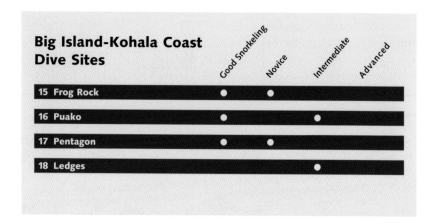

Big Island-Kohala Coast Dive Sites	Good Snorkeling	Novice	Intermediate	Advanced
15 Frog Rock	●	●		
16 Puako	●		●	
17 Pentagon	●	●		
18 Ledges			●	

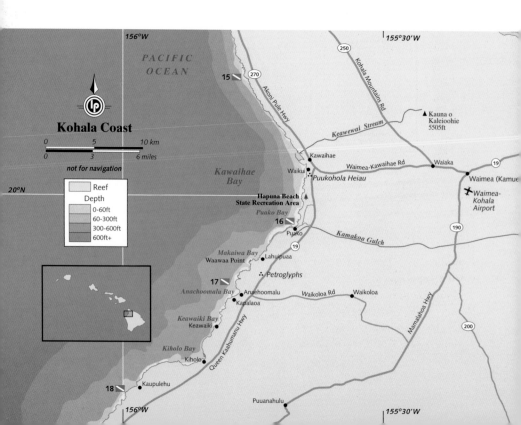

15 Frog Rock

Location: North Kawaihae Bay

Depth Range: 20-60ft (6-18m)

Access: Boat

Expertise Rating: Novice

This site, named after a rock on the shoreline that (with a little imagination) resembles a frog, is representative of north Kohala Coast diving. During your descent you'll find a lush and pristine hard-coral garden consisting mostly of finger and lobe corals.

Although reef fish are not as abundant here as they are along the Kona Coast, this site tends to be a great area to see octopuses. It takes a keen eye to find one of these masters of camouflage. They are also masters of escape, and will elude you if you don't spot them before they spot you. Look at least 30ft in front of you to catch a glimpse of one before it has the chance to make a quick exit.

As you continue southeast along the coral reef you'll find several lava caverns and swim-throughs that are inhabited by sponge crabs, cowry shells and resident whitetip reef sharks. The rocks along the floors and walls of the caverns are beautifully encrusted with red and orange sponges. Outside the caverns you'll find pufferfish, butterflyfish, filefish and other tropicals.

Frog Rock features impressive hard-coral gardens.

16 Puako

Location: Puako Bay

Depth Range: 30-90ft (9-27m)

Access: Boat or shore

Expertise Rating: Intermediate

This is an excellent dive in many respects. Several lava fingers extend from the rocky shore. Each one features spectacular archways, swim-throughs, tunnels and countless crevices. This is a great site to look for crabs, Triton's trumpet shells, cowries, nudibranchs and much more.

If you follow the lava fingers from the shore you'll eventually reach the pristine finger-coral garden that is used as a resting area by about a dozen or more green sea turtles. If you are diving from a boat, you will most likely start your dive in the coral garden and work your way up into the shallows along the finger reefs.

Schooling yellow tangs and goldring surgeonfish roam Puako's healthy finger-coral reefs.

This dive can be performed as a shore dive, but only when the weather and water are extremely calm; however, even this does not guarantee your safety. Many local divers have a "survival" story to tell about being caught in dangerous conditions while shore diving in this area, although they entered the water while it was still glassy and calm. The afternoon winds are unpredictable and make diving here potentially hazardous. Waves that are suddenly kicked up by the wind can make shore entry and exit treacherous. Additionally, to reach the water you'll need to cross over sharp volcanic rock. If you do decide to shore dive here, go early in the morning, when conditions are generally more stable. In any case, an experienced guide is highly recommended.

17 Pentagon

When conditions are favorable, this shallow dive can be very enjoyable. Located just off the stunning beach at Anaehoomalu Bay, this site features a maze of interconnected tunnels, caverns and arches. The tunnel system has five large openings, hence the name. Numerous small openings and skylights allow

Location: Anaehoomalu Bay

Depth Range: 20-30ft (6-9m)

Access: Boat

Expertise Rating: Novice

sunlight to enter into this lava maze. You'll definitely benefit from using a flashlight to see the marine life that inhabits the tunnels. Crabs, shrimps, cowries and soldierfish are among the most common resident critters, but occasionally even Spanish dancers may be seen.

When water conditions are less favorable, surge can make tunnel exploration difficult or even hazardous and penetration is not recommended. A nice coral garden surrounds Pentagon, making it

an interesting dive even if you don't enter the tunnels.

Numerous species of squirrelfish inhabit the lava caverns of Pentagon.

18 Ledges

This terrific dive is located on the Kahuwai Reef, just off the beach by the Four Seasons and Kona Village Resorts. There are two large ledges: one starts at 20ft and reaches 45ft, and the other starts at 60ft and drops below 160ft. Although it is possible to explore both ledges on one dive, divemasters often split the site into two to accommodate both novice and advanced divers.

Both ledges are characterized by sheer walls with countless overhangs and archways that are filled with crustaceans, shells and nocturnal fish such as soldierfish and squirrelfish. Whitetip reef sharks are frequently seen underneath the overhangs. Manta rays and spinner dolphins are often encountered near the shallower ledge, while the deeper ledge is home to large schools of pyramid butterflyfish, endemic bandit angelfish and even an occasional 300lb Hawaiian grouper.

Location: West of Kaupulehu

Depth Range: 20-130ft (6-39m)

Access: Boat

Expertise Rating: Intermediate

The lava arches at Ledges shelter an assortment of marine life.

Kona Coast

The Kona Coast stretches from Keahole Point to Kakio Point along the Big Island's western shore. Due to the island's massive mountains, this area experiences a sheltered lee that stretches several miles seaward and makes this one of the most desirable diving areas on the island. Calm water tends to be the norm, though during the winter months (when water conditions are more conducive to surfing) divers occasionally experience turbid water and limited visibility. About a mile offshore there is a steep drop-off where deep-water pelagics are commonly seen. The Kona Coast also boasts some of the Big Island's most pristine reefs and an abundance of exciting lava caves.

LEE FOSTER
Puuhonua o Honaunau (Place of Refuge).

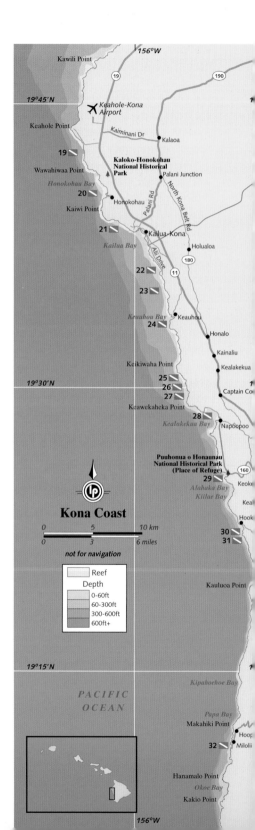

Sunset along the Kona Coast at Place of Refuge.

Big Island-Kona Coast Dive Sites

	Good Snorkeling	Novice	Intermediate	Advanced
19 Pinetrees	●	●		
20 Turtle Pinnacle	●	●		
21 Kaiwi Point	●		●	
22 Milemarker 4	●		●	
23 Kahaluu	●	●		
24 Manta Ray Village	●		●	
25 Sharkie's Cove	●		●	
26 Long Lava Tube	●		●	
27 Driftwoods			●	
28 Kealakekua Bay	●	●		
29 Place of Refuge	●	●		
30 Rob's Reef	●		●	
31 Three Room Cave				●
32 Tubastrea Tunnel				●

19 Pinetrees

Pinetrees is a large area on the north tip of the Kona Coast, and can really be divided into several dives. Due to its fascinating lava formations and abundant and diverse marine life, this is one of the most popular dive areas for dive operators

Location: South of Keahole Point

Depth Range: 15-100ft (5-30m)

Access: Boat

Expertise Rating: Novice

Pinetrees features unusual species such as this striking dragon moray.

based in Kailua-Kona or Honokohau Harbor. In the winter, the reef gets hit by the surf, creating less-than-pristine dive conditions, though divers will still encounter a wide variety of marine life.

The lava tubes and archways near the shoreline support interesting reef life, as do the seaward rubble patches. Divers can encounter a large variety of moray eels, including zebra, yellowmargin, dragon and whitemouth morays, as well as huge conger eels. This is also a great spot to observe or photograph large schools of friendly butterflyfish and bluestripe snappers. One of the most popular critters here is the frogfish, which can grow to more than a foot long. These odd-looking creatures mesmerize novice and advanced divers alike.

20 Turtle Pinnacle

This is the best site along the Kona Coast to encounter turtles. Divers will often find them resting on the rubble-covered bottom and on the finger coral near the lava ledge. Often they can be observed at a cleaner station, where yellow tangs, convict tangs and goldring surgeonfish provide their cleaning services. Swarms of these little fish pick algae and parasites off the turtle's shells, keeping them clean, healthy and streamlined while reaping

Location: Honokohau Harbor

Depth Range: 20-60ft (6-18m)

Access: Boat

Expertise Rating: Novice

the benefits of an easy meal. The turtles are accustomed to divers and completely ignore their presence, which provides many terrific opportunities to photograph these friendly marine reptiles.

The fish life in this area is replete with schooling oval chromis and butterflyfish. As you swim toward shore the terrain transitions into large boulders, where small frogfish and octopuses make their home. The shallows are also an excellent place to look for parrotfish, Christmas wrasses and surge wrasses.

Yellow frogfish may be spotted at Turtle Pinnacle.

21 Kaiwi Point

Pawai Bay is the starting point for this dive, Kaiwi Point. This bay is an excellent spot for novice divers and snorkelers due to its protection from currents and its shallow depth. The fish here are accustomed to being fed and are friendly. In fact, the multitudes of lemon butterflyfish and black durgeonfish will rush to the surface to greet you.

The bottom of the bay is covered with finger coral, rubble patches and large boulders—perfect terrain for octopuses, wrasses and parrotfish. When conditions are calm, divers can explore the small caverns, nooks and crannies along the shoreline. The cavern ceilings are encrusted with tubastrea coral. At nighttime, when the polyps open up to feed, these corals resemble beautiful flower beds. As long as conditions are calm and you stay inside the bay, this site is an excellent night dive with plenty of swimming crabs, 7-11 crabs and reef lobsters crawling out of their daytime hiding spots.

More-experienced divers will find the best diving toward

Location: Pawai Bay, south of Kaiwi Point

Depth Range: 15-130ft (5-39m)

Access: Boat

Expertise Rating: Intermediate

Kaiwi Point, the dive site's namesake. The bottom slopes quickly down beyond

Named after the number of spots on its shell, the 7-11 crab is commonly encountered on night dives.

You'll have excellent visibility at Kaiwi Point because the rugged lava coastline lacks sandy beaches. Very little sand is stirred by the wave movement, even under surgy conditions.

100ft, so be sure to watch your depth. You are likely to experience a current at the point, which in turn attracts the abundant marine life found at this spot. There is plenty of fish life, and moray eels are everywhere. If you drop down the slope a bit, you may spot unusual fish species such as flame wrasses or longfin anthias. There have been quite a few whale shark and humpback whale sightings over the years, and manta rays, eagle rays and dolphins frequent the area.

22 Milemarker 4

This dive site is popular with local divers. It is convenient and easy to find—just pull up to the side of Alii Drive at milemarker 4. When conditions are calm,

Location: South of Kailua-Kona

Depth Range: 10-60ft (3-18m)

Access: Shore

Expertise Rating: Intermediate

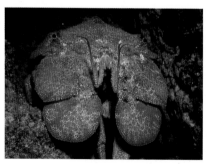

You can find shovelnose slipper lobsters during night dives at Milemarker 4.

this is an easy and enjoyable dive. To enter the water you have to walk through a shallow area that is littered with lava rocks, so when the surf is up it is best to skip this dive.

The shallow cove is also a good snorkeling spot, without the crowds of

Kahaluu (dive site 23). The best diving is to the south, in deeper water near the exit of the cove. Here, you'll find a variety of shallow canyons with nooks, crannies and overhangs. There is also a small lava chimney that can be carefully entered on calm days.

This area also makes an exceptional night dive, with an array of crustaceans that emerge from the crevices to feed.

23 Kahaluu

Although diving is possible in Kahaluu, the bay is so shallow that most people simply go snorkeling. This great spot is easily accessed by snorkelers and offers some of the best fish-watching opportunities on the Big Island.

To enter the water, follow the narrow natural channel that starts just below the lifeguard tower and winds its way through the lava rocks. Do not attempt to walk over the slippery and sharp lava rocks.

Once in the water, you are likely to encounter one of the resident sea turtles. Throughout the bay you'll find some of Hawaii's most colorful fish, including the *humuhumu nukunuku apua'a* (Picasso triggerfish), Christmas wrasses, butterflyfish and parrotfish.

On calm days you can dive outside the breakwater, but be cautious of the offshore current. It has been known to sweep divers down the coast, necessitating a rescue mission by the coast guard.

Location: South of Kailua-Kona

Depth Range: 0-20ft (0-6m)

Access: Shore

Expertise Rating: Novice (inside the bay only)

Moorish idols and colorful butterflyfish are easily approached at Kahaluu.

24 Manta Ray Village

Manta Ray Village, located in front of the Kona Surf Hotel, has become the most popular night dive in Hawaii. Every night the hotel shines powerful lights on the water, which attract plankton, which in turn attract manta rays.

Divers have seen up to 10 mantas at one time "performing" their spectacular underwater show, but it is more common to find only a couple at a time. Although there is no guarantee that mantas will show up on any night, dives during the new moon seem to be the best bets for manta encounters.

Since several dive operators anchor here every night, the bottom terrain is not particularly good, but nocturnal marine life is surprisingly abundant. Spanish dancers, sleeping parrotfish, sleeping goatfish and beautiful cowries

Location: Keauhou Bay

Depth Range: 20-40ft (6-12m)

Access: Boat

Expertise Rating: Intermediate

can all be found here, but all of these are generally outperformed by the mantas.

Snorkeling with the mantas can also be a fun and rewarding experience, but you must be aware that Manta Ray Village is in the middle of a boat channel. It is not recommended to dive or snorkel this site from shore, not only because of possible boat traffic, but also because the entrance over the sharp lava rocks can be extremely dangerous.

Watch out for boat traffic from Keauhou Bay when diving or snorkeling at Manta Ray Village.

Photographing Mantas at Night

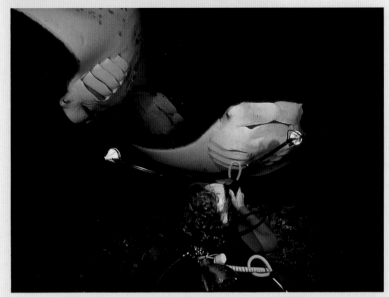

Photographing mantas at nighttime takes skill and a little luck.

Manta Ray Village presents a unique and consistently good opportunity to photograph these magnificent creatures. Once the mantas establish their feeding pattern, they tend to ignore the divers that surround them. The best way to observe and photograph the mantas is to remain somewhat stationary and allow them to approach you. Encounters within a foot or so are common. Still, there are several things that make photographing the mantas at night a challenge. Your chances of getting a good shot are much better if you are prepared with the right equipment, and know how to use it to your advantage.

Photographers will find the greatest difficulty is the low-level light at night. Pushing your film a stop or two will compensate a little for the lack of ambient light (some films are designed to be pushed up to 1000 ASA). However, you must realize that you will need to adjust your settings to compensate not only for the mantas' very reflective underbelly, but also for their black top side, which absorbs the strobe flash. It is best to choose and then shoot several times from the same basic angle and distance while bracketing to increase your chances of capturing an image with the correct exposure.

Because the dark top side of the rays contrasts little with the dark aquatic background, most auto-focus systems will have trouble. One way around this is to focus on the white underside, where you are likely to find gill slits and sometimes black spots that provide enough contrast for most auto-focus cameras to function.

You may also have difficulty composing your shots with a camera that has a small viewfinder. It can be difficult to see the partially black rays in the surrounding darkness. We recommend a manual-focus housing with a large sports viewfinder, or a Nikonos camera with a 15mm or 20mm lens and the appropriate viewfinder, along with two strobes. Set the focus to the desired distance and shoot as soon as the manta is within your focal range or depth of field.

25 Sharkie's Cove

Named after a whitetip shark that used to be seen dozing underneath one of the overhangs, this site is near Red Hill, an area distinguished by a red cinder cone that has been partly eroded by the sea. Above the red cinder, a large patch of green catches one's eye, hence the dive site is also known as Meadows.

Location: South of Keikiwaha Point

Depth Range: 25-50ft (8-15m)

Access: Boat

Expertise Rating: Intermediate

Along the shoreline you can explore several large lava tunnels, caverns and a beautiful archway, all of which provide opportunities for some nice wide-angle photographs.

A variety of crustaceans, including swimming crabs, slipper lobsters and sponge crabs, are frequently spotted inside the lava formations. Underneath the overhangs you'll find Hawaiian turkeyfish, multicolored nudibranchs and beautiful tiger cowries. Occasionally, barracuda can be observed cruising the shallows. The healthy finger reef that extends perpendicularly to the coastline is home to an abundance of reef fish. You'll find largemouth lizardfish, devil scorpionfish and octopuses residing in the areas of rubble and sand that surround the reef.

This site is one of the best night dives on the Kona Coast. After dark, the reef is literally crawling with Spanish dancers, slipper lobsters, spiny lobsters, moray eels and partridge tun shells.

Largemouth lizardfish are frequently spotted in rubble areas near reefs.

26 Long Lava Tube

Long Lava Tube is a little south of Sharkie's Cove (but still within the Red Hill area) and features one of the longest lava tubes in Hawaii. There are several skylights that allow light to penetrate through the ceiling, but overall the tube is dark enough that you may see active nocturnal species even during the day. Crabs and other crustaceans, morays and even Spanish dancers make the tube their residence. Be sure to bring your dive light to illuminate what Long Lava Tube has to offer.

Location: South of Keikiwaha Point

Depth Range: 15-50ft (5-15m)

Access: Boat

Expertise Rating: Intermediate

of marine life, as well as a large patch of rare, soft leather coral.

Outside the tube you'll find countless other lava formations that shelter critters such as conger eels, Triton's trumpet shells and schooling squirrelfish.

Take a compass reading of the sheer-sided cinder-cone cove before you start your dive. To finish your dive, swim toward this shore. You'll come across a couple of gorgeous reefs that feature an abundance

Delicate snowflake coral decorates some of the lava formations.

27 Driftwoods

This site is characterized by two lava fingers than run perpendicularly to the shore. The fingers start at a shallow plateau, where you'll find a series of caves, overhangs and other lava formations that shelter Hawaiian pipefish, and slipper lobsters, sponge crabs and other crustaceans.

The smaller of the two fingers, located to the south, starts in about 15ft of water and extends seaward until it ends abruptly with the top of the finger at 30ft

Location: North of Keawekaheka Point

Depth Range: 15-80ft (5-24m)

Access: Boat

Expertise Rating: Intermediate

and the bottom at 60ft. The other lava finger to the north provides the main attraction of the dive. It continuously drops as it extends seaward until it flattens out and blends into the finger-coral reef at 120ft.

Both lava fingers, particularly the deeper one, attract a great variety of marine life, probably due to the currents that occasionally sweep through this region. The uncommon bandit angelfish is often seen here below 70ft, along with psychedelic wrasses, bridled triggerfish and redspotted sandperches. In the shallower areas of the reef you are likely to see moray eels and perhaps even a spotted snake eel.

Use your flashlight to find critters like this shrimp in the dark overhangs at Driftwoods.

28 Kealakekua Bay

This is where Captain Cook, the "official discoverer" of the Hawaiian Islands, was killed in 1779. The spectacular backdrop of sheer lava cliffs and ancient Hawaiian burial sites makes this bay a fantastic place to visit. Below the surface, this sheltered bay is just as beautiful. Pristine coral gardens that begin in the shallows

Location: Kealakekua Bay

Depth Range: 10-130ft (3-39m)

Access: Boat

Expertise Rating: Novice (shallows only)

Snorkel and dive boats frequent Kealakekua Bay.

at 15ft and continue down to 100ft make this a wonderful site for both snorkelers and divers.

The abundant marine life includes friendly fish as well as rare species and numerous moray eels. Experienced fish-watchers will recognize the beautiful flame angelfish; saddleback, raccoon and oval butterflyfish; blacktail snapper and other rarities. This is also an excellent area to spot leaf fish, lizardfish, frogfish, turkeyfish and some of the biggest trumpetfish.

Kealakekua Bay is also home to a resident pod of dolphins, whose clicking sounds are commonly heard underwater in the winter months. Though it is rare to see a humpback whale while diving, divers can often hear them singing. Toward the point, encounters with manta rays and whale sharks are also possible.

Blue-Water Diving

Oceanic whitetip sharks roam the seas a few miles offshore.

Blessed with very calm waters and a coastline that drops quickly to several fathoms, the Kona Coast offers the unique opportunity to see pelagic species in the open ocean while blue-water diving. A few miles offshore, adventurous divers may encounter whitespotted and bottle-nosed dolphins, pilot whales, pelagic sharks, marlin and other large game fish. However, taking the plunge into the clear, blue water is not for the fainthearted. Free diving and scuba diving in blue water can be extremely hazardous due to the potential of disorientation and should not be performed without proper safety measures and professional guidance. A reference line, drift line and proper surface support are but a few of the elements necessary to safely enjoy the blue-water experience. One must keep in mind that locating marine life miles offshore can be a challenging task, leaving the best chances of success to those operators who offer blue-water adventures on a regular basis.

29 Place of Refuge

Also known as Puuhonua o Honaunau Bay, this area features Hawaii's best shore dive in regard to accessibility, coral growth and marine life. A natural lava step is used as an entrance point. Be sure that the surf is down when you enter and especially when you exit, otherwise this area can be hazardous.

Location: Puuhonua o Honaunau Bay

Depth Range: 10-120ft (3-36m)

Access: Boat or Shore

Expertise Rating: Novice (Shallows only)

Once you are in the water you'll be able to see a sandy patch to the right at 30ft where there is a big ALOHA sign made out of bricks that some energetic diver constructed years ago. To the left of the entrance area you'll find several small canyons with overhangs and many nooks and crannies. These are good areas to see crabs, moray eels and sea turtles. If you swim straight out, you'll find that the bottom drops quickly down to below 130ft. You'll find some of the most beautiful finger-coral and plate-coral formations along this drop-off.

Snorkeling is excellent in the shallow water along the edges of the bay. You will see pristine lobe-coral gardens and an abundance of surgeonfish and tangs, including inquisitive yellow tangs.

30 Rob's Reef

Rob's Reef (also known as Twin Sisters) features a vast finger-coral garden that is home to a variety of fish that tend to be less common in other areas. Brilliant flame angelfish, flame wrasses, psychedelic wrasses and smalltail wrasses are just some of the beautiful residents.

Location: South of Hookena

Depth Range: 30-100ft (9-30m)

Access: Boat

Expertise Rating: Intermediate

Two lava ridges extend at right angles from the shore to about 50ft. Start your dive along the south ridge. Once you have passed both ridges, return to the shoreline and you'll find yourself approaching a giant two-story cavern that is beautifully embellished with red, yellow and orange encrusting sponges.

Be sure to check out the coarse black sand surrounding the ridges for the unusual crocodile snake eel. These bizarre critters bury themselves in the sand, leaving only their heads exposed. Their color may range from blood-red to white.

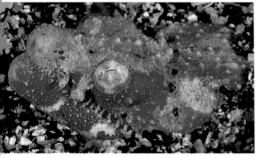

Crocodile snake eels are ambush hunters, relying on camouflage to capture prey.

31 Three Room Cave

This is one of the best cave dives along the Kona Coast. There are no skylights or windows, so expect the interior to be very dark. Though the three large, two-story-deep chambers invite divers to explore, this dive should only be made with the proper safety equipment—use a line for reference, have backup lights and have a backup tank with regulator.

In the farthest and darkest chamber, mole lobsters and candycane shrimp can sometimes be seen. Both are species that never emerge into the open light. The other chambers are inhabited by

Location: South of Hookena

Depth Range: 40-80ft (12-24m)

Access: Boat

Expertise Rating: Advanced

Hawaiian, spiny and bull's-eye lobsters, sponge crabs, cowries and many other photogenic critters. Near the entrance of the cave you may meet "Hoover," a large trumpetfish who is known to follow divers, only to suddenly dart forward and literally suck up little shrimps that are stunned by the divers' flashlight beams.

The outside of the cave is another dive in itself. The abundance of interesting critters makes this region special. Colorful harlequin shrimp can be found here, along with snake eels, hairy hermit crabs, octopuses and much more. This is definitely a dive not to be missed, but do be aware of potentially strong currents.

Harlequin shrimp can be seen on dusk or night dives.

32 | Tubastrea Tunnel

This is a spectacular dive site, but the currents can be raging, so do not attempt to approach this site from shore. Tubastrea Tunnel is situated about 600ft from shore right in front of the fishing village of Milolii, which has long benefited from the rich fishing grounds in this area.

Location: West of Milolii

Depth Range: 20-90ft (6-27m)

Access: Boat

Expertise Rating: Advanced

Underwater, at about 35ft, you'll find a huge lava tunnel that is entirely encrusted with tubastrea coral. The tunnel is open on both ends but, though it is short, the inside is only dimly lit. A flashlight is useful to get a better look at the marine life, but is not needed to find your way from end to end.

Near the tunnel, you are likely to find an incredible array of unusual cowries, nudibranchs and even frogfish. Although the tunnel is the main attraction, there are various other canyons, caverns and overhangs along the shoreline. The seafloor slopes from about 60ft to 90ft. Drop seaward down the slope and you'll likely spot a wide range of unusual critters. Dragon morays, colorful nudibranchs, snake eels, octopuses and tiger morays can all be added to this site's animal inventory.

Advanced divers will also appreciate Tubastrea Tunnel as a night dive, with the reef and tunnel walls literally crawling with interesting nocturnal critters.

A variety of nudibranchs and shelled snails can be found near this site's namesake tubastrea coral.

Photographing Lava Formations

Hawaii's many lava caverns, archways, tunnels and tubes provide exciting photo opportunities. By utilizing a strobe light, you can take advantage of the colors of the encrusting sponges and tubastrea corals and bring out their rich red, bright orange and yellow hues to produce some dazzling images.

You can also work with the natural sunlight to produce silhouetted, wide-angle and scenic shots. Many of the caverns have solid shapes, skylights or windows that lend themselves to interesting compositions and that provide good contrast. Placing the radiant sunbeams within the frame of your photograph will help to create drama, while a diver in the background will add depth to your image. Shoot at an upward angle and use a fast shutter speed of at least 1/250 to sharpen the shimmering sunbeams.

Maui County Dive Sites

Maui County includes Maui, the tiny Molokini Crater, Kahoolawe, Lanai and Molokai. Maui is renowned for its luxurious resorts and fancy restaurants, but still has plenty of unspoiled places. Perhaps it is this combination that makes the island so popular with honeymooners. Molokini Crater, the tip of an extinct volcano, rests halfway between Maui and Kahoolawe. The uninhabited island of Kahoolawe once served as a religious center for native Hawaiians, but from 1939 to 1990 it was used for live bombing and shelling, first by the U.S. Army and then by the U.S. Navy. The island is now being restored to facilitate Hawaiian cultural and spiritual activities again. Lanai is a relatively unspoiled but small and barren island that was once home to Dole's pineapple plantations. Production has ceased and the island is concentrating on attracting tourism. Molokai is still charmingly rural and slow paced and is only lightly visited by tourists.

These islands once formed a single large island, but the ocean eventually filled in the low-lying areas and separated the land into four individual land masses (with the tip of Molokini Crater still above water, too). The channels between these islands are exceptionally shallow, providing ideal breeding and nursing grounds for North Pacific humpback whales. During the winter months be on the lookout for these gentle giants while you are both above and below the water.

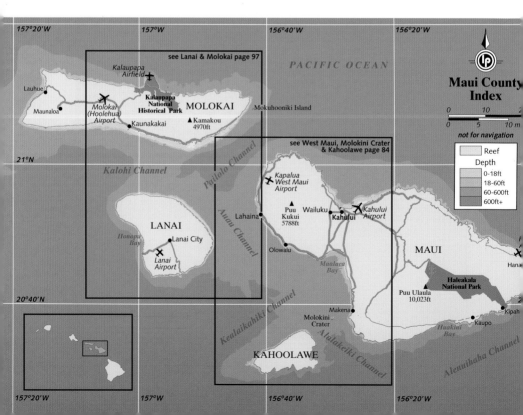

Because of Maui's proximity to its neighboring islands, chances are good that when you sign up with a dive operator based out of Maui, you'll actually end up diving at one of the other islands. For this reason, Maui County is often said to have the most diverse diving.

Though Maui has several dive sites noted for their abundant green sea turtles, the neighboring islands are home to the most exhilarating sites. Each day several dozen dive and snorkel boats voyage to the world-famous Molokini Crater. Kahoolawe's prolific fish life is occasionally visited, while some of the region's most spectacular lava caverns are found on Lanai. Finally, the island of Molokai is home to some of the wildest diving, though there are just a few days each year when dive sites are accessible.

Humpback Whale Tales

Humpback whales belong to the filter-feeding baleen whale family. Instead of bony teeth they have baleen—rigid strips made of a material similar to human fingernails—that they use to filter small fish, krill and other crustaceans out of the water.

ANDREW SALLMON

North Pacific humpback whales migrate from their summer feeding grounds near Alaska and British Columbia to winter in the Hawaiian Islands, where they reproduce, calve and nurse from October to May.

Divers most often see humpbacks at the surface spraying water from their blow-holes, or as they partake in playful tail and fin slapping. Occasionally divers are lucky enough to observe a full breach, when a whale propels up to two-thirds of its body out of the water. Divers sometimes see whales underwater, though they are more likely to hear them "singing." Whale songs are unique compositions of squeals and groans that can carry a great distance.

Humpback whales are endangered mammals and are protected throughout the Hawaiian National Marine Sanctuary. They may not be approached within 300ft (90m) by boats, divers or snorkelers.

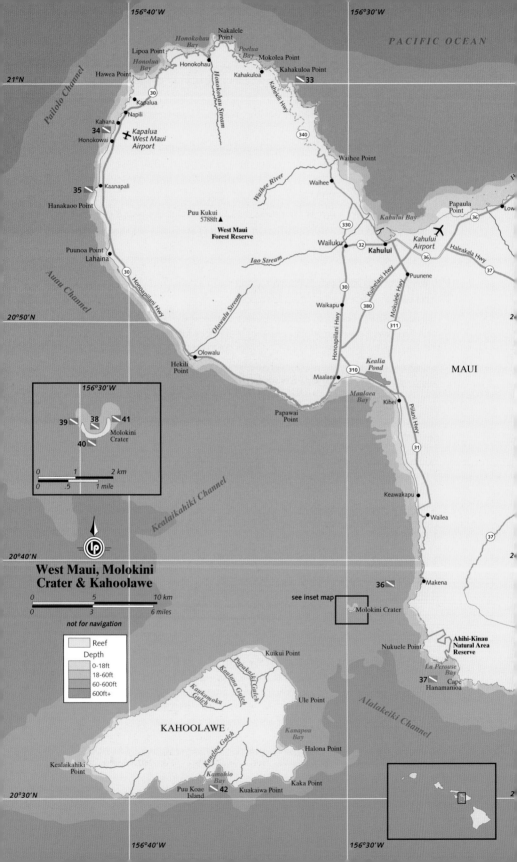

PACIFIC OCEAN

156°40'W
156°30'W

Nakalele Point
Honokohau Bay
Poelua Bay
Lipoa Point
Honolua Bay
Hawea Point
Honokohau
Mokolea Point
Kahakuloa
Kahakuloa Point
33
21°N

30
Kapalua

Napili
Kahana
34
Kapalua West Maui Airport
Honokowai

35
Kaanapali
Hanakaoo Point

Puunoa Point
Lahaina

340

Waihee Point

Waihee River
Waihee

330

Puu Kukui
5788ft ▲
West Maui Forest Reserve

Wailuku
32
Kahului
Kahului Bay
Papaula Point
Low
36
Kahului Airport
Haleakala Hwy
36
37
Puunene

Iao Stream

Honoapiilani Hwy
30
Olowalu Stream

Waikapu
380
311

Maalaea
310
Kealia Pond

MAUI

Mokulele Hwy
Kuihelani Hwy

20°50'N

Hekili Point
Olowalu

Papawai Point

Maalaea Bay

Kihei

Pailolo Channel
Auau Channel
Honoapiilani Hwy

156°30'W

39
38
41
40
Molokini Crater

0   1   2 km
0   .5   1 mile

Kealaikahiki Channel

Keawakapu
Pilani Hwy
31

Wailea
37

20°40'N

**West Maui, Molokini
Crater & Kahoolawe**

0   5   10 km
0   3   6 miles

not for navigation

Reef
Depth
0-18ft
18-60ft
60-600ft
600ft+

36
Makena

see inset map
Molokini Crater

Nukuele Point
Ahihi-Kinau Natural Area Reserve
La Perouse Bay

Kuikui Point

Papakaiki Gulch
Kaulana Gulch
Kaukamoku Gulch

Ule Point

37
Cape Hanamanioa

KAHOOLAWE

Kanoloa Gulch

Kanapou Bay

Halona Point

Alalakeiki Channel

Kealaikahiki Point

Kamohio Bay
Puu Koae Island
42
Kuakaiwa Point
Kaka Point

20°30'N

156°40'W
156°30'W

Maui

Maui, the second largest Hawaiian island, arose from the ocean floor as two separate volcanoes. Lava flows and erosion eventually built up a valley-like isthmus between the two, linking them in their present form. The southeastern portion of Maui is dominated by Haleakala, and the northwest by Puu Kukui. The two high peaks block the trade winds that blow in from the northeast.

You'll find Maui's best and most consistently good dive sites along the leeward shore that winds down from Kaanapali to La Perouse Bay. Although the north shore is Maui's longest coastline, this region is seldom dived due to its remoteness and year-round rough water. However, on a calm day, the diving here can be well worth it. The windward southeast coast is rarely visited because of near-constant winds, swells and strong currents.

Bird's-eye view of Maui's coastline.

Maui, Molokini Crater & Kahoolawe Dive Sites	Good Snorkeling	Novice	Intermediate	Advanced
33 Hidden Pinnacle				●
34 Black Rock	●	●		
35 Hyatt Reef	●	●		
36 Five Caves	●		●	
37 La Perouse	●		●	
38 Inside Crater	●	●		
39 Reef's End			●	
40 Back Wall				●
41 Enenue			●	
42 Puu Koae			●	

33 Hidden Pinnacle

Hidden Pinnacle, with its steep drop-offs and big-fish action, is a good example of Maui's wild, spectacular diving. Unfortunately, due to its location on the windward (northeast) side of the island, the area is generally too rough to dive. On those few days when kona conditions (southern winds) prevail, divers can venture out to the pinnacle, which rises from 120ft to the surface.

Location: Southeast of Kahakuloa Point

Depth Range: 0-120ft (0-36m)

Access: Boat

Expertise Rating: Advanced

The pinnacle is home to large schools of pyramid butterflyfish and endemic oval chromis, and is covered with soft leather coral (a species otherwise rarely seen in Hawaii) and lush blankets of colorful sponges. When there is a current, you are likely to see pelagic animals such as trevallies, wahoos or tunas cruising by.

Pyramid butterflyfish can often be seen schooling at Hidden Pinnacle.

34 Black Rock

Black Rock is probably not the most thrilling shore dive on Maui, but it is the easiest, safest and most convenient. A large, black volcanic-rock peninsula juts out several hundred feet from the other-

Location: Southwest of Kahana

Depth Range: 15-30ft (5-9m)

Access: Beach

Expertise Rating: Novice

A variety of tang species, such as this stunning sailfish tang, can be seen here.

wise sandy shore in front of the Sheraton Hotel. The south side of the peninsula borders and protects the bay, which is a perfect playground for novice divers and snorkelers. The area is also a popular night dive that is suitable for all levels of divers.

The underwater terrain consists mostly of sand and volcanic rock, and marine life highlights include a large variety of friendly fish. Expect to be approached by large swarms of butterflyfish and tangs. They are used to being fed and their approach provides good snapshot opportunities in very shallow water.

If you are a more experienced diver you may want to leave the cove, which is easiest to do near the reef along the peninsula. You'll be rewarded with better visibility and more-natural marine life behavior, but be prepared for a moderate current once you reach the peninsula's point.

35 Hyatt Reef

This reef is not far offshore in front of the Hyatt Regency Hotel, but is too distant to be reached from the beach. The highlight here is the resident green sea turtles, which are so accustomed to divers that they tend to ignore them. You'll generally find the turtles resting on the rubble-covered bottom, on the finger coral or on their way to the surface to take a breath of air. These turtles make great photo opportunities, but please don't ride, touch or harass the animals. Green sea turtles are protected and there are hefty fines for disturbing these animals in any way.

The dive site consists of several reef areas interspersed with patches of sand. You may find cone shells, helmet shells or little sand gobies. As you drop deeper the coral turns into a rubble area where octopuses are commonly seen. You may also see devil scorpionfish, rockmovers and spottail dartfish. As you learn to identify these critters, the apparently barren rubble suddenly becomes much more interesting. This site also features several large antler-coral trees that often host the endemic whitespot damselfish. As you drop down the slope a bit, watch out for potentially strong currents.

Location: West of Kaanapali

Depth Range: 40-50ft (12-15m)

Access: Boat

Expertise Rating: Novice

Green sea turtles are residents of Hyatt Reef.

36 Five Caves

This site is called both Five Caves and Five Graves. Either way, you can't go wrong. It features several caves and caverns, and is located in front of a cemetery of five Japanese graves that marks the dive's entry point.

Although this dive site is frequently visited by dive boats, it is also a quality shore dive for experienced divers. The entrance is a rocky one, so be cautious! Because this area has become popular for launching kayaks and small powerboats, it can sometimes get a little crowded.

From shore, swim through the natural channel to reach the dive site. Swim just past the wash rocks (the partially submerged rocks that get washed over when the surf is up) and then descend to the two lava fingers that run perpendicularly to the shore. These lava formations are punctuated by a series of caverns, arches

Location: West of Makena

Depth: 40ft (12m)

Access: Boat or shore

Expertise Rating: Intermediate

and overhangs filled with crimson Hawaiian bigeye fish, soldierfish and crustaceans. Divers frequently report encounters with turtles, moray eels and conger eels and occasionally even white-tip sharks.

This site is also a popular night dive. If you are planning a nighttime shore dive, you should be very familiar with night diving logistics. Avoid shore diving here, especially at night, or whenever any wave action is present.

Five Caves is characterized by numerous caves, caverns and overhangs.

Night Diving

Hawaii boasts some of the best night diving in the world. After dark, the reefs come alive with an awesome diversity of crustaceans and other critters that are hidden in the lava caverns, nooks and crannies during the day. Many of them are brilliantly colored, such as the flame-orange Hawaiian and bull's-eye lobsters, the multicolored regal slipper lobster, the scarlet Spanish dancer, the Hawaiian swimming crab and many others.

Spanish dancers hide during the day and feed on sponges at night.

Night diving provides macro photographers with an excellent opportunity to get close to their subjects. Most reef fish are found in a dormant state in and around the coral, which allows you to closely observe and photograph many species that are skittish during the day. You will also notice that many of the fish take on different, more somber color patterns at night.

There is no need to penetrate caves and lava tubes, since most of the nocturnal creatures will be roaming the open reef. Moray eels are commonly encountered hunting for their prey, while cowries can be observed in the open, utilizing their mantles as camouflage.

If you are shooting with a Nikonos system, you will find a close-up kit or a 1- to 2-macro extension setup to be very rewarding. Utilizing a fixed 1-to-1 macro lens such as a 60mm or 105mm lens can also produce outstanding results. Be sure to rig a spotter flashlight onto your system so that you don't find yourself shorthanded. Aiming the light beam directly at the animal may cause it to retreat. Photographers generally fare best when the subject is lit by only the outer glow of the light.

37 La Perouse

This dive site is located in the middle of the scenic La Perouse Bay, found at the end of Makena Alanui Road. The bay is a fairly recent creation in Maui's geological history, formed by a lava flow about 200 years ago. A lava-rock pinnacle runs perpendicularly to the shoreline, rising from the seafloor at 60ft to 10ft below the surface. Located approximately ¼ mile from shore, the pinnacle requires a bit of a swim and

Location: La Perouse Bay

Depth Range: 10-60ft (3-18m)

Access: Boat or shore

Expertise Rating: Intermediate

diving here can only be recommended when conditions are calm.

Most divers first notice the abundance of slate pencil urchins, one of the few urchin species that is not only very pretty but also harmless to divers. The shallows also often harbor Triton's trumpet shells along with a variety of sea stars. The fish are very friendly here, and divers can even approach the timid bird wrasse.

You can explore several nice caverns inhabited by squirrelfish and bigeye fish. Check smaller crevices for crabs, ghost shrimp or banded coral shrimp. Out in the open you are likely to see endemic bluestripe butterflyfish, banded angelfish, flame angelfish and schools of goatfish and perhaps turtles. La Perouse is one of the sites in Hawaii where you may also encounter a barracuda or two and, if you swim out to the site's most seaward point, you could get lucky and catch a glimpse of spinner dolphins cruising by.

Divers discover a crown-of-thorns sea star in the shallows at La Perouse.

Molokini Crater

The tip of this extinct volcanic crater rises out of the water in the channel between Maui and the uninhabited island of Kahoolawe. The northern side has been breached by the ocean. The southern half of the crater is still intact, creating a crescent-shaped island of volcanic rock that is barely ¼ mile (400m) long. The crater can be divided into four main diving areas: the inside, the outside and the two points of the crescent.

Molokini is a designated marine life conservation district. All boats visiting Molokini use moorings rather than anchors to keep coral damage to a minimum, but the high volume of divers has certainly affected the reef. If you like to avoid crowds, try to find an operator that visits Molokini in the afternoon. Tour operators occasionally offer two morning dives on the outside of Molokini, then move to the inside after most other boats have left.

38 Inside Crater

This is by far Maui County's most popular spot for snorkeling, snuba and scuba diving. The inside of the crater is almost always protected from the wind and current, is accessible year-round and is suitable for all levels of divers and snorkelers. The bottom's mix of rubble and sand with scattered rock and reef formations provides an ideal habitat for a variety of species. There are zillions of butterflyfish, saddle wrasses, chubs, surgeonfish, parrotfish and bluestripe snappers that fearlessly approach both

Location: Molokini Crater

Depth Range: 10-30ft (3-9m)

Access: Boat

Expertise Rating: Novice

divers and snorkelers. Octopuses, moray eels, leaf fish and other friendly critters can also be found within the crater's sheltered cove.

At Inside Crater lemon butterflyfish and orangeband surgeonfish swarm divers and snorkelers.

39 Reef's End

Reef's End is an excellent site for more-experienced divers. This dive usually starts on the inside edge of the northern, submerged part of the crater. Establish your neutral buoyancy and work your way around the point toward the outside of the crater, where visibility is generally much better than inside.

Location: Molokini Crater

Depth Range: 60-100ft (18-30m)

Access: Boat

Expertise Rating: Intermediate

The topography here consists of huge lava slabs and large boulders that are beautifully encrusted with red sponges. This site also features massive antler coral swirling with damselfish. You'll find many mated pairs of butterflyfish, including the less common oval (also called redfin) butterflyfish and saddleback butterflyfish. As you come around the point, keep your eyes open for whitetip reef sharks.

This is also a good site to encounter a variety of eels, many of which are accustomed to divers. Many will poke their heads out of their holes when divers are near. Though some can be closely approached, beware that not all eels are diver-friendly. Keep a healthy respect for these wild animals to ensure a safe dive.

Curious yellowmargin morays may poke their heads out of holes as you approach.

ANDREW SALLMON

Deep Diving

Opportunities to dive deep abound in Hawaii. Many attractions are beyond 130ft (40m), the recognized maximum depth limit of sport diving. Before venturing beyond these limits, it is imperative that divers be specially trained in deep diving and/or technical diving.

Classes will teach you to recognize symptoms of nitrogen narcosis and proper decompression procedures when doing deep or repetitive deep dives. Remember, emergency facilities in Hawaii are limited and can be difficult to reach. Know your limits and don't push your luck when it comes to depth.

40 Back Wall

The Back Wall (also called the Outside Wall) of the crater is a spectacular experience and rates as one of the best dives in Hawaii. The dramatic black, sheer crater wall with its colorful sponges, schooling fish and often crystal-clear water is simply a breathtaking dive.

Location: Molokini Crater

Depth Range: 0-130ft (0-39m)

Access: Boat

Expertise Rating: Advanced

Due to the makeup of the site and drift driving logistics, the Back Wall is only suitable for fairly experienced divers. Since the wall drops vertically from the surface to way beyond recreational depth limits, perfect buoyancy control is a necessity.

Covered with red and orange encrusting sponges, the wall boasts several black-coral trees, wire corals and endless nooks and crannies that often contain critters such as cowries, shrimps, nudibranchs and even long-handed lobsters. Particularly noticeable are the colorful fish that naturally form large schools, unlike the solitary fish in other popular locations that look for handouts from divers. You are likely to see large swirls of pennant, raccoon and pyramid butterflyfish. Reef sharks and larger pelagic fish such as wahoos and tunas are also commonly seen.

Large schools of pennant butterflyfish are common at Back Wall.

41 Enenue

Enenue is the Hawaiian name for rudder-fish. This site is named for its abundance of these silver gray members of the sea chub family, which are generally looking for a handout when they rush to greet you.

Although the beginning of this dive is pretty easy, it becomes more challenging as you follow the southern inside crater wall toward the point. The base of the crater wall levels off to a wide shelf. Here you should look for octopuses, moray eels and the unusual snake eel. If you have keen eyes, you may spot a rare boarfish. The shelf eventually plummets deeper than 130ft. If you continue along the wall toward the often current-swept point you have a good chance of seeing big fish such as tunas, mantas, and

Location: Molokini Crater

Depth Range: 50-130ft (15-39m)

Access: Boat

Expertise Rating: Intermediate

wahoos. There have also been reports of whale shark sightings in this area.

When you are diving off of an anchored boat, it's usually best to turn around once you reach the point, but the dive could also be performed as a drift dive, in which case you could continue around the point and dive along the crater's back wall until your gauges indicate that it's time to come up.

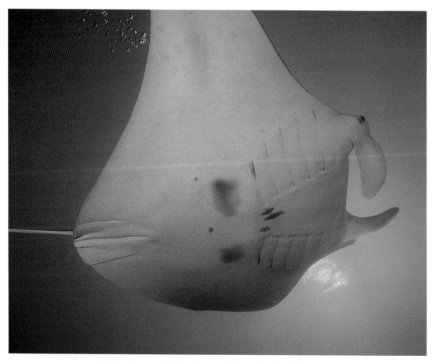

Lucky divers might spot a manta soaring by at Enenue.

Kahoolawe

Kahoolawe is an uninhabited island just 7 miles (11km) off the southwest coast of Maui. Though once a green and forested island, it is now largely barren due to overgrazing. All cattle were moved off the island when it was leased in 1939 to the U.S. Army for bombing practice. Kahoolawe is slowly recovering from this half-century of target practice and live-shell bombing. You may occasionally encounter live ammunition or shells on a dive, so watch for debris and be careful. Though the reefs here are partially damaged due to the bombing, the fish life is prolific.

42 Puu Koae

This is one of Kahoolawe's best sites, located at a small rock island off the south shore. If you are an underwater photographer with a housed camera or simply a diver that enjoys finding unusual fish, you will probably appreciate this site.

Location: Puu Koae Island

Depth Range: 40-100ft (12-30m)

Access: Boat

Expertise Rating: Intermediate

The seaward side of the rock island quickly drops to 100ft, then turns into a boulder terrain that gradually slopes below 130ft. This type of underwater environment generally supports many different species and you may find longfin anthias, fire dartfish, bandit angelfish or Tinker's butterfly-fish throughout the bouldery landscape. At 50ft you'll find a cave waiting to be explored. If you use a flashlight, you'll be able to find the abundant lobsters inside.

When diving around Kahoolawe, remember it was once used for bombing and target practice. At this site, be sure to avoid the inshore side of the small island, since live ammunition still scatters the heavily bombed seafloor.

Fire dartfish are occasionally seen within the boulders of Puu Koae.

Lanai

Lanai lies 9 miles (14km) south of Molokai and 9 miles (14km) west of Maui. *Lanai* means "hump" in Hawaiian; when viewed from Maui, the island looks somewhat like the back of a whale rising out of the water. The dramatic cliffs and barren landscape are distinct characteristics of the island. Though Lanai was formerly used for ranching and plantations, it is now transitioning to luxury resorts.

Divers will find spectacular underwater caves, caverns and tunnels along Lanai's south coast, which offers the best and most protected diving on the island.

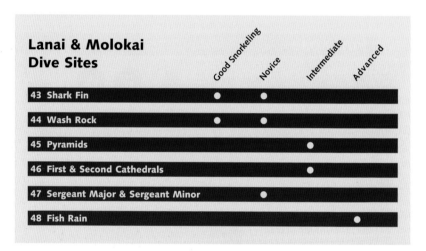

Lanai & Molokai Dive Sites	Good Snorkeling	Novice	Intermediate	Advanced
43 Shark Fin	●	●		
44 Wash Rock	●	●		
45 Pyramids			●	
46 First & Second Cathedrals			●	
47 Sergeant Major & Sergeant Minor		●		
48 Fish Rain				●

43 Shark Fin

A lava formation that resembles a shark's dorsal fin protruding through the surface of the water marks this site. The underwater terrain consists mostly of lava rock, with a lava finger running perpendicularly from shore. Generally, the dive starts at the fin-shaped rock and you slowly make your way along its submarine extension, which is characterized by jagged lava that conceals a great amount of marine life within its nooks and crannies.

Due to frequent currents flowing through this area, you'll find one side of the rock beautifully embellished with orange cup coral and vast blankets of red encrusting sponges. It is also an excellent spot to locate moray eels and octopuses.

Location: Northwest of Palaoa Point

Depth Range: 20-90ft (6-27m)

Access: Boat

Expertise Rating: Novice

Although coral growth is sparse, this site is popular with snorkelers due to the large school of lemon butterflyfish that rush to the surface to greet them. If you are an accomplished free-diver, it's fun to dive down along the fin rock to see the same colorful scenery that divers enjoy.

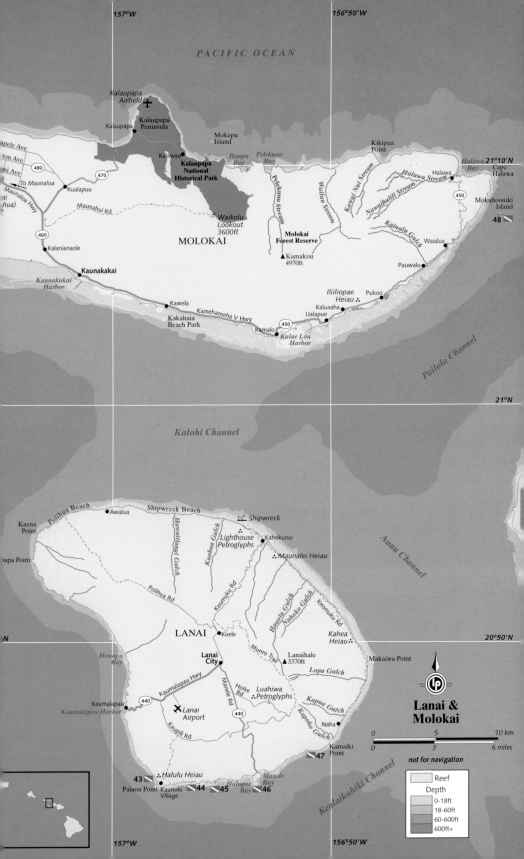

PACIFIC OCEAN

157°W 156°50'W

*Kalaupapa
Airfield*
Kalaupapa
Kalaupapa
Peninsula
Kalaupapa
Kalawao
**Kalaupapa
National
Historical Park**

*Mokapu
Island*

*Haupu
Bay* *Pelekunu
Bay*

Kikipua
Point

21°10'N
*Halawa
Bay*
Halawa
Halawa Stream
Cape
Halawa
450
*Mokuhooniki
Island*

48

Wailau Stream
Kawela Nui Stream
Nawaihulili Stream

Kainalu Gulch

Waialua

Pauwalu

Apele Ave
ton Ave
mi Ave
480
To Maunaloa
Kualapuu
470
*Maunaloa Hwy
(hua)*
Maunahui Rd

460
Kalanianaole

Kaunakakai

*Kaunakakai
Harbor*

MOLOKAI

*Waikolu
Lookout
3600ft*

Pelekunu Stream

**Molokai
Forest Reserve**

▲ *Kamakou
4970ft*

*Iliiliopae
Heiau* ⛩

Pukoo
Kaluaaha
Ualapue
Kawela
Kamehameha V Hwy
Kakahaia
Beach Park
450
Kamalo
*Kalae Loa
Harbor*

Pailolo Channel

21°N

Kalohi Channel

Kaena
Point

Polihua Beach
Awalua
Shipwreck Beach
⚓ Shipwreck
Lighthouse
Petroglyphs
Kahokunui

Maunalei Heiau

Auau Channel

apa Point

Hawaiiloqui Gulch
Kuahua Gulch

Polihua Rd
Keomuku Rd

LANAI
Koele

Munro Trail

Hawola Gulch
Nahoko Gulch
Keomuku Rd

*Kahea
Heiau* ⛩

20°50'N

N

*Honopu
Bay*

**Lanai
City**

*Lanaihale
3370ft* ▲

Lopa Gulch

Makaiwa Point

Kaumalapau
440
Kaumalapau Harbor

Kaumalapau Hwy

Manele Rd

✈ *Lanai
Airport*
440

*Hoike
Rd*

*Luahiwa
Petroglyphs*

Kapua Gulch

Kapoho Gulch

Naha

Ⓛⓟ

**Lanai &
Molokai**

0   5   10 km
0   3   6 miles

not for navigation

Kaupili Rd

43

⛩ *Halulu Heiau*
Palaoa Point   Kaunolu
Village
44

45

*Hulopoe
Bay*

*Manele
Bay*
46

Kamaiki
Point

47

Kealaikahiki Channel

| Reef |
| Depth |
| 0-18ft |
| 18-60ft |
| 60-600ft |
| 600ft+ |

157°W 156°50'W

44 Wash Rock

Wash Rock is a great dive with lots of variety and color. This large lava pinnacle barely protrudes above the surface and its tip is often awash in the break of the swells. Perhaps it is due to this constant water movement that the upper part of the pinnacle is blanketed with a variety of colorful sponges. A small school of blue-stripe snapper are often found dashing in and out of the overhangs. With the varied color and ample light you will find many excellent photo opportunities.

A short swim will bring you to the "tunnel of love," a lava tube where you are

Location: South Lanai

Depth Range: 0-60ft (0-18m)

Access: Boat

Expertise Rating: Novice

likely to find a mated pair of yellowmargin moray eels. The area outside the tunnel is great to poke around in and interesting critters are often found. Inquisitive divers may even spot an elusive octopus.

There are a variety of overhangs to explore at Wash Rock.

45 Pyramids

From lava arches and pinnacles to expanses of finger corals and reef fish, Pyramids is a diver's playground. Named for the great number of schooling pyramid butterflyfish commonly found at the top of the pinnacles, Pyramids offers some of Lanai's best diving.

From the mooring, a short swim south takes you to a large, hollow lava pinnacle. The numerous nooks and crannies in the sides of the pinnacle shelter a high concentration of marine life. Schools of bluestripe snapper swim near the soft snowflake and black corals. Lobster and cleaner shrimp hide behind the thick swarms of nocturnal squirrelfish that will part in the beam of your dive light. Several eels also make their home here, including sizable yellowmargin moray eels and the vicious-looking viper moray. Shy pipefish hide in small cracks and, if you are lucky, you may be able to view a sleeping whitetip reef shark.

Leaving the pinnacle, you can find lava arches about 120ft to the west. These swim-throughs are laced with pretty snowflake coral. Lobsters, crabs and large cowry shells can often be found in the

Location: South Lanai

Depth Range: 40-80ft (12-24m)

Access: Boat

Expertise Rating: Intermediate

archways. Throughout the dive site, solitary barracuda can be spotted.

There are sand channels another 40 yards west that offer helmet shells, peacock flounder and the sand-diving razor wrasse. Pyramids is a dive site that was only recently discovered but is quickly becoming a favorite.

The archways are home to stunning orange-banded cowries.

46 First & Second Cathedrals

First and Second Cathedrals, Lanai's most famous and certainly most spectacular dive sites, are located along the island's south shore. First Cathedral is about 3 miles east of Second Cathedral. These sites feature huge, two-story-high underwater grottoes.

Both grotto systems consist of arches, tunnels, ridges and passageways that are sensational to explore. Inside the grottoes you'll find rich marine life that

Location: Southeast of Hulopoe Bay

Depth Range: 20-65ft (6-20m)

Access: Boat

Expertise Rating: Intermediate

includes lobsters, crabs, cowries and bright-red soldierfish.

You can enter First Cathedral through a tunnel leading into a huge chamber that provides divers with a spectacular light show. When the sun is out, light enters the chamber through the porous lava ceiling. The sun's laser-like rays dance through the interior, reminiscent of a cathedral's stained glass windows.

Enter the Second Cathedral through a wide crack in a wall. There are two main chambers whose ceilings are blanketed with tubastrea coral; a black-coral tree hangs down from the ceiling of one of the chambers. Light also enters the cavern through side cracks, but it is not as dramatic a show as in First Cathedral.

Though the grottoes are accessible most of the year, be especially cautious in the shallow areas that have ceiling holes if there is any surge present. The water funneling through can flash you through the water or bang you into the sharp lava formations.

A dramatic underwater grotto at Second Cathedral.

Safe Diving in Lava Caves

Many of Hawaii's top dive sites center on the region's unique and exciting lava formations, created when molten lava flowed into the ocean. The outer layer of the lava flow cooled and solidified when it came into contact with the water, creating hollow tubes, tunnels, archways and a multitude of caves and caverns. These fascinating formations (now home to an array of marine life) are usually a diver's dream, but can quickly turn into a nightmare if safety concerns are ignored.

Strong surge, loss of light, disorientation and complicated interconnecting tunnel systems can be serious hazards for divers. A diver should only consider cave penetration when accompanied by an experienced guide who is familiar with the cavern. Consult with your dive guide on any special safety equipment that may be needed and, of course, whether conditions are safe to dive.

When entering an overhead environment, divers should adjust their buoyancy to be slightly negative to reduce the effect of any sudden surge movement. Always move slowly and keep plenty of space between you and the diver in front of you to avoid having your mask kicked off or your regulator pulled out of your mouth by their fins. The less finning, the better; if you must kick, simple foot-ankle movements are best. Remember, if you don't feel comfortable entering overhead environments, there is nothing wrong with staying behind, preferably with a dive buddy, and enjoying the outside of the cave.

47 Sergeant Major & Sergeant Minor

Sergeant Major is a great dive site for divers who like to poke around, look into every hole and peek under every ledge. There is a ton of marine life on this dive, as well as interesting topographic formations. Three ridges run seaward, two of which are connected by a beautiful archway. You may occasionally see whitetip reef sharks near the archway or the ridges. You will also see the usual tropical fish and turtles found throughout the region.

A large sandy area separates Sergeant Major from its counterpart, Sergeant Minor. The latter's claim to fame is a 50ft-long lava tube with a huge (but friendly) moray eel slinking around somewhere inside. If you get the chance to take a close look at the eel, be sure to check for cleaner shrimp that may be

Location: Southwest of Kamaiki Point

Depth Range: 25-50ft (8-15m)

Access: Boat

Expertise Rating: Novice

present on or around its face. These cleaner shrimp are known for their bravery and their ability to clean a multitude of teeth in a very short period of time.

Both Sergeant Major and Sergeant Minor face the open ocean, so be sure to at least occasionally turn your eyes to the deeper water—large game fish, dolphins and (from October through May) humpback whales may be seen cruising the area.

A multitude of tropical fish is found at Sergeant Major and Sergeant Minor.

Molokai

This rural, slow-paced island offers little tourist hype to accompany its deserted beaches, spectacular valleys, and historical sites. All of Molokai's dive sites are located around the small offshore island Mokuhooniki. Due to its lack of protection from wind and waves, dive sites are accessible only on perfectly calm days, which are rare. The area is subject to very strong currents and dives are usually performed as drift dives. Only advanced divers should sign up to go diving at Molokai.

48 Fish Rain

Fish Rain is perhaps Molokai's most exhilarating dive, with dense schools of fish constantly cruising overhead. You are likely to see more fish here than on most other dives in Hawaii.

Another large attraction is the possible sighting of "serious" pelagic animals. Hammerhead sharks, tiger sharks, whale sharks, humpback whales and monk

Location: Mokuhooniki Island

Depth Range: 80-130ft (24-39m)

Access: Boat

Expertise Rating: Advanced

seals have all been seen at this site at one time or another.

The site itself is along the outer slope of an underwater cinder cone that rises from 150ft to the surface of the water. This site can only be accessed when weather and water conditions permit the boat-crossing from Maui. Even when the crossing can be made, currents may be very strong on this dive.

You may see humpbacks at this dive site.

Kalaupapa

On Molokai's central north shore lies the Kalaupapa Peninsula, surrounded on three sides by some of Hawaii's roughest waters and on the fourth side by the world's highest sea cliffs. It was here that lepers were sent into exile to prevent the spread of leprosy, which was introduced to the Hawaiian Islands during the 19th century. Father Damien, a Catholic missionary, arrived at Kalaupapa in 1873. He erected more than 300 dwellings, installed a water system and nursed the sick until he succumbed to the disease himself in 1889.

Since the 1940s, sulfone antibiotics have controlled leprosy (now called Hansen's disease) successfully, and all of the fewer than 100 patients are free to leave. But Kalaupapa Peninsula is the only home this older population knows and most choose to stay. Today, tourists may visit the peninsula, but they are required to take a guided tour to minimize their impact on this community.

Kauai & Niihau Dive Sites

Covered by lush tropical forest, Kauai is aptly nicknamed the "Garden Island." With stunning scenery and scant development, it is a mecca for hikers, kayakers and other adventurers. Niihau, Kauai's closest neighbor, is generally referred to as the "Forbidden Island." This small, dry, windswept island has been privately owned since 1864. Limited numbers of non-Hawaiians are permitted to visit.

When weather conditions are favorable, Kauai and Niihau offer some unique and exciting dive opportunities. The islands' position on the northern edge of the warm-water coral belt and the fact that their shorelines are prone to large swell impacts mean that corals are not as abundant as they are along the southern Hawaiian Islands. What the region lacks in coral reefs it makes up for with exciting lava formations, unusual fish species and pristine diving conditions.

LEE FOSTER

The dramatic Na Pali Coast can be explored by boat or helicopter.

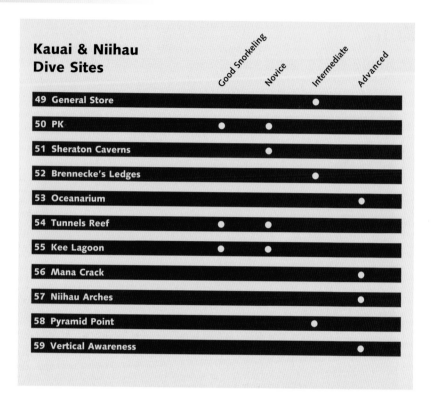

	Good Snorkeling	Novice	Intermediate	Advanced
49 General Store			●	
50 PK		●	●	
51 Sheraton Caverns			●	
52 Brennecke's Ledges			●	
53 Oceanarium				●
54 Tunnels Reef		●	●	
55 Kee Lagoon		●	●	
56 Mana Crack				●
57 Niihau Arches				●
58 Pyramid Point			●	
59 Vertical Awareness				●

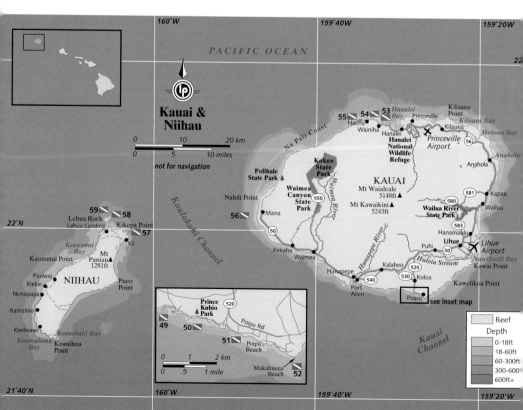

Kauai

Kauai is the fourth largest of the Hawaiian Islands, with an area of 558 sq miles (1,445 sq km). If you are looking for lush scenery, this is the place to be. The North Shore is green and mountainous, with waterfalls, beautiful beaches and stream-fed valleys. The northwest coast is lined by the steeply fluted Na Pali sea cliffs, Hawaii's foremost hiking destination. Though summer trade winds keep the heat down, Kauai's climate changes more with location than season and tends to be more varied than the other islands.

Excellent dive sites are found around the island, but overall, access is less reliable than the rest of the Hawaiian Islands because of Kauai's less-predictable weather conditions. Sites located along the dramatic North Shore are undiveable during the winter months, and even the south shore spots can be sketchy at times. Although there are good novice dive spots on Kauai, some of the prime sites are better suited to more experienced divers.

49 General Store

Located on Kauai's south shore, this site is so named because it has something of interest for everyone. It is home to the remains of the steamship *Pele*, which sank on March 25, 1895 after running aground on Kalaniupao Rock about ¼ mile away. Unfortunately, Hurricane Iniki scattered the already battered pieces of the wreck, but you can still recognize the propeller, several anchors and some of the ground tackle.

The site is perhaps most noteworthy for its wide variety of marine life. Along the seaward side of a large U-shaped ledge are three large lava caves cradling rare critters such as brilliantly colored ghost shrimp and Hawaiian pipefish. Pipefish are small, elongated fish that—due to their cryptic habits and camouflaging abilities—are rarely seen. Once spotted, they tend to be quite approachable.

Along the wall, you'll find several black-coral trees that are home to longnose hawkfish, a popular macro-photographer's subject. You can also see large schools of the endemic lemon

Location: West of Kukuiula Bay

Depth Range: 50-80ft (15-24m)

Access: Boat

Expertise Rating: Intermediate

You can expect to see large schools of bluestripe snapper at General Store.

butterflyfish, bluestripe snapper and perhaps turtles and whitetip reef sharks.

50 PK

Named after its location just offshore from Prince Kuhio Kalaniana'ole's birthplace near Poipu Beach, PK is an ideal site for novice divers. The shallow depth, lack of current and relative protection from wave action make the site well suited for divers' first Open Water dives. The interesting lava formations and abundance of marine life ensure that more-experienced divers also enjoy this site.

There are countless nooks and crannies where you may find pretty shells or colorful shrimp. Friendly reef fish are

Location: West of Prince Kuhio Park, Poipu

Depth: 20ft (6m)

Access: Shore

Expertise Rating: Novice

seen throughout the dive, including rainbow-hued parrotfish, brilliantly colored butterflyfish and elegant angelfish.

51 Sheraton Caverns

Also known as The Circus, this dive has become one of Kauai's most popular sites for novice and advanced divers alike. It's conveniently located near Poipu Beach, enjoys relative protection from the swells and offers lots to see.

Three huge lava tubes run perpendicularly to the shoreline in front of the

Location: Poipu Beach

Depth Range: 35-65ft (11-20m)

Access: Boat

Expertise Rating: Novice

Outside the tubes you may find a rare leaf fish.

Sheraton Kauai Hotel in Poipu. Both the inside and outside of the tubes are an underwater photographer's heaven. Upon entering the tubes, look for spiny lobsters, reef crabs, 7-11 crabs and shrimp. Maybe you'll even find a Spanish dancer or turkeyfish hiding inside.

Be sure to take a good flashlight and don't forget to check out the ceilings. Turkeyfish and crustaceans are often found hiding upside down in the crevices of the lava ceilings. Outside the tubes you may find yellowmargin and whitemouth moray eels, friendly sea turtles and even rare critters such as leaf fish or giant anglerfish.

52 Brennecke's Ledges

Brennecke's Ledges (also known as Brennecke's Drop-Off) is located on Kauai's southeast shore, just east of Poipu off of Makahuena Point. A large lava shelf runs parallel to the shore for several miles. Its prime feature is a wall that drops down to 90ft. The top of the black lava shelf is beautifully studded with white and pink cauliflower coral. This area is always worth checking out for large Triton's trumpet shells, pincushion sea stars and small hermit crabs that often seek shelter within the protective branches of the coral.

Location: Makahuena Point

Depth Range: 60-90ft (18-27m)

Access: Boat

Expertise Rating: Intermediate

for lobsters, reef crabs, squirrelfish and even whitetip reef sharks that may be dozing underneath the overhangs. Schooling bluestripe snappers and green sea turtles may also be encountered at this site.

As you drop down the wall, you'll find several black-coral trees and possibly endemic banded angelfish. Be sure to examine the numerous overhangs with your flashlight. You'll find that many of the ceilings are entirely covered with the brightly colored orange cup coral. There are several types of nudibranchs that feed on the cup coral and can often be found among the individual polyps. You may see another resident, the stunning orange-banded cowry. Be sure to look

Underneath the overhangs you may encounter a dozing whitetip shark.

Wreck of the *Luckenbach*

The *Andrea F. Luckenbach* was a 400ft freighter that hit a reef and sank off Kauai's east coast on March 4, 1951. Time and weather have taken their toll on the wreck, and the chains, 10ft anchors, propeller and boiler-room pieces are now scattered across the ocean floor. Squirrelfish and bigeyes seek shelter in the wreckage, and snapper and goatfish swim in mid-water nearby.

Though the wreck can be dived from shore, the distance and unpredictable conditions make reaching it a challenge, and visibility is limited. The *Luckenbach* should not be dived without a professional guide. Local dive operators may offer shore dives to the wreck from December to February.

53 Oceanarium

For advanced divers, Oceanarium is one of Kauai's most exciting dives. Located on the North Shore not far from the Na Pali Coast, the site is accessible only during the summer months when the seas are very calm.

Location: Hanalei Bay

Depth Range: 60-130ft (18-39m)

Access: Boat

Expertise Rating: Advanced

You'll find three huge pinnacles that start at about 65ft and drop down to 120ft in front of a lava shelf. Large, dense schools of bluestripe snapper and other fish hover in the channels between the shelf and the pinnacles.

On the seaward side of the largest pinnacle, a sheer wall plummets beyond 130ft. This is perhaps the most dramatic area, where you'll find some beautiful black-coral trees. Use a flashlight to capture the color of the black coral and the treasures they hide. Longnose hawkfish with their stunning red-and-white-checker pattern are often found within the branches.

The overhangs along the wall are encrusted with flower-like orange tube coral and may contain giant hairy hermit crabs or other crabs, nudibranchs and cowry shells. In the smaller *pukas* (crevices) along the wall look for the rare, endemic long-handed lobsters that favor this environment. This is also a great area to spot rare fish species such as morwongs and whiskered boarfish.

There's much to explore here but this is a deep dive, so be sure to check your time. Don't just rely on your dive guide to monitor your gauges: you are ultimately responsible for yourself. There is still plenty to see in the shallower areas, and if you look out into the blue you'll probably spot some uluas, barracuda or even manta or eagle rays.

Pyramid butterflyfish congregate near large black-coral trees at Oceanarium on Kauai's North Shore.

Cleaning Stations

Observant divers will find a variety of symbiotic relationships throughout the marine world—associations in which two dissimilar organisms participate in a mutually beneficial relationship.

One of the most interesting relationships is found at cleaning stations, places where one animal (or symbiont) advertises its grooming services to potential clients with inviting, undulating movements. Often this is done near a coral head or coral bommie.

Various species of cleaners such as wrasses and shrimp are dedicated to caring for their customers, which may include fish of all sizes and species. Larger fish such as sharks and mantas generally frequent cleaning stations that are serviced by angelfish, butterflyfish and larger wrasses. Turtles generally utilize the services of algae-feeding tangs that are eager to rid them of their algae buildup.

Customers hover in line until their turn comes. When the cleaner attends to a waiting customer—perhaps a grouper, parrotfish or even moray eel—it may enter the customer's

mouth to perform dental hygiene, and even exit through the fish's gills. Although the customer could have an easy snack, it would never attempt to swallow the essential cleaner. The large fish benefit from the removal of parasites and dead tissue, while the little wrasses are provided with a meal.

Divers will find that if they carefully approach a cleaning station, they'll be able to get closer to many fish than is normally possible and observe behavior seen nowhere else on the reef.

Double bar goatfish with cleaner wrasse.

ANDREW SALLMON

54 Tunnels Reef

Unfortunately, due to high surf conditions, this popular shore diving and snorkeling spot is only accessible during the summer months. You'll find the best area to enter the water at the very end of a dirt road off of Highway 56. There is a sign for this turnoff that says, "Right of way to beach."

If you are a new or less experienced diver you should keep to the right, where you'll find a large sandy area surrounded by a coral reef. Here, the bottom slopes

Location: Hanalei Bay

Depth Range: 20-65ft (6-20m)

Access: Shore

Expertise Rating: Novice

down to only about 25ft, making it an ideal spot for novices to explore the reef overhangs and lava caverns and tunnels.

If you are an experienced diver, swim to the left where the seafloor bottoms out at about 65ft. As you follow the contour of the bottom, you'll come across several ledges, caves and overhangs along with a good range of fish life. With luck you may encounter one of the resident whitetip reef sharks or sea turtles. In the sandy and rubble-covered patches you may find the unusual flying gurnard fish, razor wrasses and dragon wrasses. You are likely to experience a strong current here, which intensifies as you go deeper.

55 Kee Lagoon

Located on Kauai's North Shore just west of Haena Beach Park, this site can only be dived in the summer months when conditions are calm. The shallow central area inside the lagoon is a perfect snorkeling spot with beautiful lobe-coral formations, lots of friendly fish and many juveniles that seek the shelter of the bay.

If you are scuba diving, your best bet is to dive along either the left or the right side of the lagoon, where the water

Location: West of Hanalei Bay

Depth Range: 10-30ft (3-9m)

Access: Shore

Expertise Rating: Novice

is a little deeper. If you are a novice diver you should keep to the right, where currents are mostly absent. In either direction you are likely to see schooling convict tangs (called *manini* in Hawaiian), butterflyfish and triggerfish, but to the left you'll find more ledges and a good variety of critters.

On extremely calm days, experienced divers can swim through the lagoon and descend along the outside of the fringing reef. The water tends to be very clear out here and is filled with caves, overhangs and a great abundance of fish.

LEE FOSTER

Kee Lagoon's sandy beaches provide easy access for divers and snorkelers.

56 | Mana Crack

Mana Crack is one of Kauai's more exciting but weather-dependent dives and is only likely to be accessible during the summer months. Located near the dramatic Na Pali Coast, this site offers unusual terrain consisting of a reversed ledge that is deeper near shore and shallower on the seaward side.

Location: Southwest of Nahili Point

Depth Range: 50-95ft (15-29m)

Access: Boat

Expertise Rating: Advanced

Expect to see some gorgeous coral formations, including plate and antler corals, along with rare black-coral trees. Use your flashlight to explore the countless overhangs and small *pukas* (crevices) for lobsters, hermit crabs and cowry shells. Although there's never a guarantee, you may encounter at least some of the resident "big boys" such as eagle rays, blacktip reef sharks and possibly even hammerhead sharks.

Mana Crack boasts beautiful antler coral.

Niihau

The island of Niihau, located 17 miles (27km) southwest of Kauai, is the smallest of the main inhabited Hawaiian Islands. It earned the nickname the "Forbidden Island" when it was closed to all but native Hawaiians in 1864 (when the island was privately purchased). Restrictions have become more lax and visitors are now allowed to take helicopter tours of the island.

A limited number of dive boats are also able to access the island's waters. A 1- to 1½-hour channel crossing is necessary to reach Niihau and the nearby Lehua Rock, a slightly larger and more exciting version of Maui's Molokini Crater. Both Niihau and Lehua Rock boast breathtaking drop-offs, gigantic sea arches, canyons, and caverns, most of which are best suited to advanced divers.

57 Niihau Arches

Perhaps Niihau's most popular and thrilling site, Niihau Arches gets its name from its principal feature—an immense archway at 35ft amid an "underwater city" of ridges, valleys and lava tubes. The largest tube extends into a huge chamber that is about 100ft square. Longnose hawkfish inhabit the black feather coral and regular black coral found interspersed throughout the lava formations.

Location: East Kikepa Point

Depth Range: 20-80ft (6-24m)

Access: Boat

Expertise Rating: Advanced

The site quickly drops as you swim out, providing an excellent area to watch large fish swim by: eagle rays, pelagic sharks (such as the occasional Galápagos shark), blacktip sharks and wahoos are among the site's visitors. If you are familiar with local fish species, you'll notice that this pristine site also boasts an abundance of otherwise rare fish, such as morwongs, and is an excellent place to observe octopuses.

With some luck, you may even be able to observe a playful Hawaiian monk seal. These endemic mammals are highly endangered and under no circumstances should they be touched or harassed in any way.

Monk seals are occasionally seen at Niihau dive sites.

58 Pyramid Point

Pyramid Point—which lies opposite Vertical Awareness at Lehua Rock—is a fantastic wall that drops vertically from 18ft to about 180ft (below the recreational dive limit). This site is generally an easy drift dive where you can often see mantas, sharks, eagle rays and even Hawaiian monk seals. Although monk seals are curious and have been known to approach divers, be sure to keep a respectful distance and never chase or attempt to touch these rare, endangered mammals.

After you have used up your bottom time along the wall, slowly work your way back up to the top of the wall. From there, cruise through the channel between the wall and Lehua Rock on the steady tidal current. When timed right, this is a great thrill, with pyramid butterflyfish, pennant and lemon butterflyfish swirling all around you.

Location: Lehua Rock

Depth Range: 18-130ft (5-39m)

Access: Boat

Expertise Rating: Intermediate

Hawaiian spiny lobsters make interesting macrophoto subjects.

59 Vertical Awareness

This site is one of the most thrilling and awe-inspiring sites in Hawaii. Advanced dive skills are a must when exploring this sheer-sided seamount that rises vertically from 280ft until it levels out at 40ft. The best features are found between 50 and 100ft. Be sure to maintain neutral buoyancy throughout the dive and be aware of your depth at all times. The water is generally gin-clear, making depth perception very deceiving.

Along the wall you are likely to encounter dense schools of pennant butterflyfish, pyramid butterflyfish and tangs. The brilliantly hued endemic Hawaiian anthias and longfin anthias are regularly seen here.

Location: Lehua Rock

Depth Range: 40-130ft (12-39m)

Access: Boat

Expertise Rating: Advanced

In addition to its small reef gems, this site is also well known for its big fish: graceful mantas, Galápagos sharks, huge uluas, wahoos, tunas and even Hawaiian monk seals all thrive in this environment. Be sure to periodically glance into the blue in order not to miss these large pelagic animals.

Midway Islands Dive Sites

Midway Islands are geographically part of the Hawaiian archipelago, but they are an unincorporated possession of the U.S., not part of the U.S. state of Hawaii. Best known as the site of a pivotal WWII battle between Japanese and American naval forces, Midway is the only northwestern Hawaiian island group open to tourism. The four islands—Sand, Gooney, Spit and Eastern—are also referred to as Midway

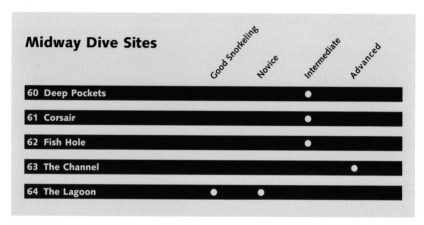

Midway Dive Sites	Good Snorkeling	Novice	Intermediate	Advanced
60 Deep Pockets			●	
61 Corsair			●	
62 Fish Hole			●	
63 The Channel				●
64 The Lagoon	●	●		

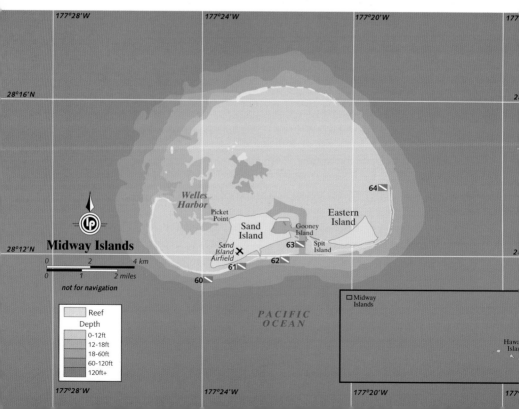

Atoll or simply Midway. All amenities (three restaurants, a small store, accommodations, dive services, and medical facilities) are on Sand Island. Visitors must pre-arrange accommodations through the Midway Phoenix Corporation, and are encouraged to book diving and fishing charters ahead of time.

The dive sites found around Midway Islands differ greatly from those found in the rest of the Hawaiian Islands because they lack developed coral formations.. Midway is located 1,050 nautical miles (1,995km) northwest of Kauai in a region where the water is too cold during the winter for coral to survive. The diving in Midway is seasonal, with winter months too unpredictable to run dive charters regularly. From May to October Midway attracts adventurous divers and those seeking the unusual. Cavern formations, an abundance of sharks and a high concentration of unusual fish species are Midway's diving attractions, which delight divers, fish-watching enthusiasts and marine biologists alike.

After being closed to the public for 50 years, Midway has evolved from a critical war outpost to a nature reserve that is managed by the U.S. Fish and Wildlife Service. Though Midway was a WWII battle site, don't expect to dive lots of naval wrecks in this area. Most of the fighting took place about 120 miles (193km) offshore, and any wrecks are now under 15,000ft (4,572m) of water.

60 Deep Pockets

This dive typifies Midway's underwater landscape. Numerous caverns, ridges, ledges and overhangs near the boat mooring provide interesting scenery and are a perfect environment for lobsters, squirrelfish and the peculiar whiskered boarfish. Thick-lipped jacks mingle with schooling yellowstripe goatfish and sea chubs, and morwongs gather in schools.

Location: Outside of southern barrier reef

Depth Range: 60-80ft (18-24m)

Access: Boat

Expertise Rating: Intermediate

The endemic masked angelfish is very common here. Wrasses and parrotfish found throughout the Hawaiian Island chain are much more common in Midway and generally double or triple the size of their Hawaiian cousins. Endemic longfin anthias, which in Hawaii are only found in depths below 120ft, are commonly seen here at 60ft.

On this dive you never need to venture far from the mooring to encounter all the action. The top of the reef is at 60ft, with most of the dive taking place around 80ft. Be sure to monitor your bottom time. As with many dive sites throughout Hawaii, this is an excellent opportunity to utilize nitrox to extend your bottom time.

61 Corsair

The wreck of this WWII plane rests on the sandy bottom at 115ft. Though the plane is broken up (only the fuselage and wing section remain), the main attraction here is the concentration of unusual and rare fish species: brilliant Japanese angelfish, colorful Schlegel's grouper, masked angelfish, Thomson's anthias, weedy scorpionfish and other species most divers have never seen before. Keep an eye out as you descend and ascend, and you may see a few Galápagos sharks circling the wrecks. This spot is a fish-photographer's heaven since all these species are gathered within inches of each other.

Location: South of Sand Island

Depth: 115ft (35m)

Access: Boat

Expertise Rating: Intermediate

Due to the small size of the wreck, only small groups should dive here. If you are nitrox-certified, you can dive this site on nitrox to extend your bottom time. Of course, be sure to use the appropriate blend for a depth of 115ft.

The Corsair is home to many unusual fish species, such as this rare Japanese angelfish.

Battle of Midway: A Vital Role for a Tiny Atoll

The Battle of Midway was arguably the single most significant conflict of WWII, as it turned the tide of war to America's favor and toward the eventual Japanese defeat. However, as with many military battles, if a few key events had progressed less favorably for the U.S., the outcome of the war might have been entirely different.

In the months preceding the battle, the Japanese advanced quickly and with little opposition throughout the Pacific. Conquering Midway would offer them a strategic outpost in their eastward progression. They hoped a confrontation would draw the remaining American battleships and aircraft carriers into a decisive battle, one the Japanese had far-superior forces to fight—and win. The Japanese, however, had not anticipated that the Americans would break their naval code and intercept a message about their surprise-attack plans.

On June 4, 1942, the Americans lay in ambush to the northeast of Midway. The battle began early in the morning on that decisive day, just five months after the attack on Pearl Harbor. The Japanese struck first, attacking the island with more than 100 planes, but the prepared American forces defended themselves well. The Japanese lost more than a third of their planes and pilots, and did little significant damage to the U.S. military. The losses forced the Japanese to halt the launch of additional aircraft that would have searched for enemy surface ships, and compelled them to re-arm planes for an additional air raid on Midway.

As the Japanese returned to their carriers after the air raid, the Americans sent troops toward the Japanese ships. Due to poor communication among the American pilots and the fact that the Japanese had moved their ships from the expected position, the first wave of the American attack was poorly coordinated and the loss of American lives and planes was heavy. While the American pilots engaged the Japanese defense fighters at sea level, the American Dauntless dive-bombers targeted the three refueling and re-arming Japanese carriers. Nearly defenseless, the Japanese carriers were sunk within minutes. At no time in naval history has a single battle turned so quickly. This day signaled the beginning of the end of Japanese control over the Pacific.

The Corsair is one of the few WWII wrecks around Midway Islands that is accessible to divers.

62 Fish Hole

Fish Hole's underwater landscape is similar to Deep Pockets', but Fish Hole is a shallower dive, allowing for more bottom time. This dive features a number of rocky outcroppings and other rock structures that contain crevices, small caverns and overhangs of various sizes scattered across the bottom—areas that attract whiskered boarfish, schooling morwongs and even huge lobsters that will venture into the open during daylight. You may also see schools of brilliantly hued crosshatch triggerfish, which are curious and will readily approach divers.

A sandy area surrounding the rock structures is home to schooling goatfish

Location: South of Sand Island

Depth Range: 50-60ft (15-18m)

Access: Boat

Expertise Rating: Intermediate

and Hawaiian stingrays. The sandy expanse slopes down gradually, so you'll have to travel a long way to get much deeper than 60ft. The relatively shallow depth and usual lack of current make this site suitable for less-experienced divers. Most of the time this is a likely location to encounter Galápagos sharks and green sea turtles.

Schooling morwongs are found throughout Fish Hole.

63 The Channel

The Channel was created by the U.S. Navy to allow large ships to pull up to Midway's wharves. Although there is a wreck of unknown origin that shelters a few fish and nudibranchs of interest, the underwater scenery is, for the most part, quite barren.

Location: Between Sand and Eastern Islands

Depth: 50ft (15m)

Access: Boat

Expertise Rating: Advanced

Galápagos sharks will be seen most clearly during an incoming tide at The Channel.

The "big boys" that frequent the channel are the main attraction here: Galápagos sharks and mantas are very common. However, the presence of Galápagos sharks can be a little nerve-racking, especially if there is an outgoing tide creating murky water conditions and low visibility. This dive is best as a drift dive during an incoming tide, when the water is clearest.

64 The Lagoon

The Lagoon is where Midway's best snorkeling is found, though it is really too shallow to dive unless you just want to explore the shallows. Snorkelers are transported by boat to a swimming platform that allows you to easily enter and exit the water.

Location: Inside of eastern barrier reef

Depth Range: 10-20ft (3-6m)

Access: Boat or shore

Expertise Rating: Novice

The shallow lagoon tends to warm up more quickly than other diving areas in Midway, providing more comfortable water temperatures for snorkelers and also allowing some coral to thrive here. A variety of tropical fish (including huge pastel-colored parrotfish) can be observed, while encounters with eagle rays are commonly reported.

Parrotfish grazes on coral at The Lagoon.

Marine Life

The warm waters surrounding the Hawaiian Island chain are home to an incredible number of fish, coral and mammal species. Due to the archipelago's isolation, approximately 30% of the reef fish and many invertebrates are endemic (found nowhere else in the world). These unique critters, along with Hawaii's fascinating lava tubes and beautiful hard-coral gardens, are part of what makes diving in Hawaii special. The animals pictured here are just a sample of the common vertebrates and invertebrates you are likely to see around Hawaii and Midway. Endemic species are listed separately.

Common names are used freely but are notoriously inaccurate and inconsistent. The two-part scientific name is much more accurate. This system is known as binomial nomenclature—the method of using two words (shown in italics) to identify an organism. The first word is the *genus*, into which members of similar species are grouped. The second word, the *species*, is the finest detail name and generally includes only organisms that can produce fertile offspring. Where the species or genus is unknown, the naming goes to the next known (and less specific) level: Family (F), Order (O), Class (Cl) or Phylum (Ph).

Common Vertebrates

green sea turtle
Chelonia mydas

humpback whale
Megaptera novaengliae

spinner dolphin
Stenella longirostris

arc-eye hawkfish
Paracirrhites arcatus

bicolor anthias
Pseudanthias bicolor

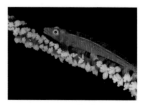

wire coral goby
Bryaninops yongei

120

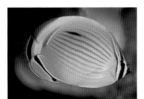

redfin butterflyfish
Chaetodon trifasciatus

fourspot butterflyfish
Chaetodon quadrimaculatus

ornate butterflyfish
Chaetodon ornatissimus

yellow tang
Zebrasoma flavescens

Moorish idol
Zanclus cornutus

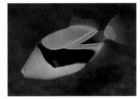

Picasso triggerfish
Rhinecanthus rectangulus

bluelined snapper
Lutjanus kasmira

yellowtail coris
Coris gaimard

broom filefish
Amanses scopas

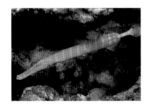

trumpetfish
Aulostomus chinensis

peacock flounder
Bothus mancus

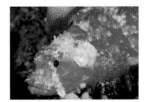

decoy scorpionfish
Iracundus signifer

leaf scorpionfish
Taenianotus triacanthus

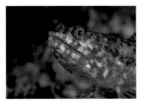

variegated lizardfish
Synodus variegatus

stout moray
Gymnothorax eurostus

Common Invertebrates

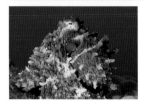

day octopus
Octopus cyanea

pimpled basket
Nassarius papillosus

reticulated cowry
Cypraea maculifera

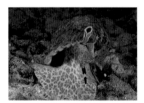

Triton's trumpet
Charonia tritonis

tiger cowry
Cypraea tigris

7-11 crab
Carpilius maculatus

mole lobster
Palinurella wieneckii

Hawaiian lobster
Enoplometopus occidentalis

tufted spiny lobster
Panulirus penicillatus

Spanish dancer
Hexabranchus sanguineus

spiny sea cucumber
Stichopus chloronotus

fried egg nudibranch
Phyllidia varicosa

slate pencil urchin
Heterocentrotus mammillatus

Christmas tree worm
Spirobranchus giganteus

cauliflower coral
Pocitlopora meandrim

Endemic Species

Hawaiian monk seal
Monachus schauinslandi

Hawaiian turkeyfish
Pterois sphex

saddle wrasse
Thalassoma duperrey

whitesaddle goatfish
Parupeneus porphyreus

Hawaiian sergeant major
Abudefduf abdominalis

threespot chromis (juvenile)
Chromis verater

filefish
Ph. *Cantherhines*

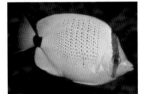
lemon butterflyfish
Chaetodon miliaris

Potter's angelfish
Centropyge potteri

regal slipper lobster
Arctides regalis

Hawaiian spiny lobster
Panulirus marginatus

Hawaiian swimming crab
Charybdis hawaiiensis

vibrating nudibranch
Chromodoris vibrata

finger coral
Porites compressa

snowflake octocoral
Anthelia edmondsoni

Hazardous Marine Life

Marine animals almost never attack divers, but many have defensive and offensive weaponry that can be triggered if they feel threatened or annoyed. The ability to recognize hazardous creatures is a valuable asset in avoiding accident and injury. The following are some of the potentially hazardous creatures most commonly found in Hawaii.

Hydroid

Though hydroids come in many forms, in Hawaii you'll find only feather and fern hydroids, which grow on reefs and in crevices. They resemble tiny plants or feathers and generally look quite fragile and harmless; however, they can "sting" by discharging small, specialized cells called nematocysts. Contact causes a burning sensation that lasts for several minutes and may produce red welts on the skin. Do not rub the area, as you will only spread the stinging particles. Cortisone cream can reduce the inflammation and antihistamine cream is good for killing the pain. Serious stings should be treated by a doctor.

Cone Shell

Do not touch or pick up cone shells. These mollusks deliver a venomous sting by shooting a tiny poison dart from their funnel-like proboscis. Stings will cause numbness and can be followed by muscular paralysis or even respiratory paralysis and heart failure. Immobilize the victim, apply a pressure bandage, be prepared to use CPR, and seek urgent medical aid.

Scorpionfish

In Hawaii, you don't have to concern yourself with deadly stonefish, but there are several types of scorpionfish, well-camouflaged creatures that have poisonous

spines along their dorsal fins. They are often difficult to spot since they typically rest quietly on the bottom or on coral, looking more like rocks. Practice good buoyancy control and watch where you put your hands. Scorpionfish wounds can be excruciating. To treat a puncture, wash the wound and immerse in nonscalding hot water for 30 to 90 minutes. Administer pain medications if necessary.

Lionfish

Also known as turkeyfish or firefish, these slow, graceful fish extend their feathery pectoral fins as they swim. They have distinctive vertical brown or black bands alternating with narrower pink or white bands. When threatened or provoked, lionfish may inject venom through dorsal spines that can penetrate booties, wetsuits

and leather gloves. The wounds can be extremely painful. If stung, wash the wound and immerse in nonscalding hot water for 30 to 90 minutes. Administer pain medications if necessary.

Moray Eel

Moray eels are very common on Hawaiian reefs. Distinguished by their long, thick, snake-like bodies and tapered heads, moray eels come in a variety of colors and patterns. Don't feed them or put your hand in a dark hole—eels have the unfortunate combination of sharp teeth and poor eyesight and will bite if they feel threatened. If you are bitten, don't try to pull your hand away suddenly—the teeth slant backward and are extraordinarily sharp. Let the eel release it and then surface slowly. Treat with antiseptics, antitetanus and antibiotics.

Sea Urchin

Sea urchins tend to live in shallow areas near shore and come out of their shelters at night. They vary in coloration and size, with spines ranging from short and blunt to long and needlesharp. The spines are the urchin's most dangerous weapon, easily able to penetrate neoprene wetsuits, booties and gloves.

There are a great variety of sea urchins in Hawaii. Many, but not all, have sharp spines. Divers should be most wary of the venomous spiny urchin, locally known as *wana*. They are generally black or black and white and have very long, brittle spines that break off easily. Puncture wounds immediately cause a throbbing pain. Treat minor punctures by extracting the spines and immersing wound in nonscalding hot water. More serious injuries require medical attention.

Crown-of-Thorns

This large sea star may have up to 23 arms, although 13 to 18 are more commonly observed. Body coloration can be blue, green or grayish with the spines tinted red or orange. The spines are venomous and can deliver a painful sting even if the animal has been dead for two or three days. Also beware the toxic pedicellariae (pincers) between the spines, which can also cause severe pain upon contact. To treat stings, remove any loose spines, soak stung area in nonscalding hot water for 30 to 90 minutes and seek medical aid. Neglected wounds may produce serious injury. If you've been stung before, your reaction to another sting may be worse than the first.

Jellyfish

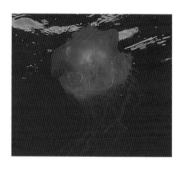

The waters of Hawaii have no strongly toxic jellyfish. Jellyfish sting by releasing the stinging cells contained in their trailing tentacles. As a rule, the longer the tentacles, the more painful the sting. Stings are often irritating and not painful, but should be treated immediately with a decontaminant such as vinegar, rubbing alcohol, baking soda, papain, or dilute household ammonia. Beware that some people may have a stronger reaction than others, in which case you should prepare to resuscitate and seek medical aid.

Portuguese Man-o-War

This colonial organism, distantly related to the jellyfish, is found at the surface, and is recognizable by its purplish, translucent "floats" and long, trailing tentacles. Its tentacles, which can reach 50ft (15m) or more in length, are armed with

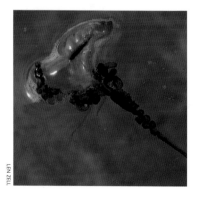

exceedingly toxic stinging cells, which can cause a painful sting. Beached man-o-wars are still hazardous, even weeks after they've dried out and appear dead. Sting symptoms range from a mild itch to intense pain, blistering, skin discoloration, shock, breathing difficulties and even unconsciousness. If stung, apply a decontaminant such as vinegar, papain or dilute ammonia and seek immediate medical aid. Allergic reactions can be severe and life-threatening.

LEN ZELL

Diving Conservation & Awareness

Hawaii's coral reefs are generally in good condition but several factors threaten the reefs and their surrounding marine life. Among these are pollution, runoff from agricultural regions and golf courses, overfishing and aquarium fish collection.

Coral-reef communities are not Hawaii's only environmental concern. Offshore, pelagic blue sharks are caught by the commercial fishing nets and longlines set to catch tuna and swordfish. It is a common practice to remove the sharks' fins (for soup, for instance) and throw the carcasses back into the water. Though the National Marine Fisheries Service (NMFS) has banned shark finning in the Atlantic Ocean, the Gulf of Mexico and the Caribbean Sea, this practice is still legal in Hawaii. Conservationists are working to protect blue sharks and other species from such offshore shark "harvesting," and are also fighting to keep commercial interests from exploiting inshore and reef shark populations.

Surprisingly, Hawaii has relatively few protected marine life areas, which means tropical fish collecting and fishing (with spears, nets or poles) are legal in most areas. The beauty and biological diversity of Hawaii's waters are at risk as a result.

Fish Collecting: A Deadly Practice

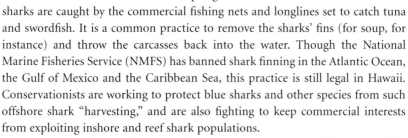

Most tropical fish and invertebrates are not bred in captivity but are collected from the ocean to supply private aquarists and commercial aquariums. Over-collection has depleted numerous Hawaiian reefs, and many species are now rarely seen by divers. Fish-collecting methods often indiscriminately destroy coral and other marine creatures, and many non-aquarium fish that are caught and released die from stress or injury. Still other fish die during transport, and those that survive the trip have a much shorter life span than fish left in their natural environment. Everyone (though particularly divers) should think twice before supporting an industry that threatens to deplete the very resource they enjoy.

The Lost Fish Coalition was established with the goal of banning tropical-fish collection. If you would like to join or find out how you can help, write to Lost Fish Coalition, P.O. Box 390508, Kailua-Kona, HI 96739.

Marine Reserves & Regulations

There are some places where fish collecting, fish feeding and spearfishing are not permitted, or are at least restricted. These areas are referred to as FMAs (Fisheries Management Areas) or MLCDs (Marine Life Conservation Districts). Though the two are very similar, FMAs tend to be less strict and to focus on protecting fish by regulating collection and fishing. Fish feeding may not be regulated and coral is generally not protected. FMAs are usually located in non-diving areas such as harbors, wharves and freshwater areas, and there are numerous FMAs throughout the islands.

The following regions are designated MLCDs: Hanauma Bay (Oahu); Pupukea (Oahu) covering the dive sites Three Tables and Shark's Cove; Waikiki Beach (Oahu) near Diamond Head; Kealakekua Bay (Big Island); Lapakahi (Big Island) along the north Kohala Coast; Waialea Bay (Big Island) on the south Kohala Coast; Old Kona Airport (Big Island); Molokini Crater (Maui); Honolua-Mokuleia Bay (Maui) along the northwestern coast; and Manele-Hulopoe Bay near the Manele Boat Harbor (Lanai).

Certain species are protected by law. On Midway Islands, several beaches are off-limits to people and are reserved for the endangered Hawaiian monk seals. The green sea turtles are also protected by law, and you can be fined for touching, feeding or otherwise bothering them. The Hawaiian Islands have been designated a National Marine Sanctuary to protect the winter breeding and calving grounds of the endangered North Pacific humpback whale. Boats, divers and snorkelers are forbidden to approach these whales closer than 300ft (90m).

Conservation efforts continue with the creation and expansion of protected areas. For example, a bill was passed that would protect approximately 30% of the Kona and Kohala coastlines from fish collecting and fishing if successfully enforced; however, enforcement is one of the greatest challenges facing all protected areas. Enforcement agencies do not always have the staff or other resources to effectively patrol protected areas. Until additional funding is provided, this will continue to be a challenge.

How You Can Help

Contact the Division of Aquatic Resources for current information and specific regulations on protected areas:

Oahu ☎ 587-0100	Maui ☎ 243-5294
Big Island ☎ 974-6201	Kauai ☎ 274-3344

You can assist enforcement efforts by reporting any violations you observe to the Conservation and Resources Enforcement Agency (part of the Department of Land and Natural Resources). To make a report, dial ☎ 0 and ask the operator for Enterprise 5469 (toll free), or dial ☎ 587-0077 (Oahu). You will receive half of the imposed and collected fines if the party is found guilty.

Responsible Diving

Dive sites tend to be located where the reefs and walls display the most beautiful corals and sponges. It only takes a moment—an inadvertently placed hand or knee, or a careless brush or kick with a fin—to destroy this fragile, living part of our delicate ecosystem. By following certain basic guidelines while diving, you can help preserve the ecology and beauty of the reefs:

1. Never drop boat anchors onto a coral reef and take care not to ground boats on coral. Encourage dive operators and regulatory bodies in their efforts to establish permanent moorings at appropriate dive sites.

2. Practice and maintain proper buoyancy control and avoid over-weighting. Be aware that buoyancy can change over the period of an extended trip. Initially you may breathe harder and need more weighting; a few days later you may breathe more easily and need less weight. Tip: Use your weight belt and tank position to maintain a horizontal position—raise them to elevate your feet, lower them to elevate your upper body. Also be careful about buoyancy loss: as you go deeper, your wetsuit compresses, as does the air in your BC.

3. Avoid touching living marine organisms with your body and equipment. Polyps can be damaged by even the gentlest contact. Never stand on or touch living coral. The use of gloves is no longer recommended: gloves make it too easy to hold on to the reef. The abrasion caused by gloves may be even more damaging to the reef than your hands are. If you must hold on to the reef, touch only exposed rock or dead coral.

4. Take great care in underwater caves. Spend as little time within them as possible, as your air bubbles can damage fragile organisms. Divers should take turns inspecting the interiors of small caves or under ledges to lessen the chances of damaging contact.

5. Be conscious of your fins. Even without contact, the surge from heavy fin strokes near the reef can do damage. Avoid full-leg kicks when diving close to the bottom and when leaving a photo scene. When you inadvertently kick something, stop kicking! It seems obvious, but some divers either panic or are totally oblivious when they bump something. When treading water in shallow reef areas, take care not to kick up clouds of sand. Settling sand can smother the delicate reef organisms.

6. Secure gauges, computer consoles and the octopus regulator so they're not dangling—they are like miniature wrecking balls to a reef.

7. When swimming in strong currents, be extra careful about leg kicks and handholds.

8. Photographers should take extra precautions as cameras and equipment affect buoyancy. Changing f-stops, framing a subject and maintaining position for a photo often conspire to prohibit the ideal "no-touch" approach on a reef. When you must use "holdfasts," choose them intelligently (i.e., use one finger only for leverage off an area of dead coral).

9. Resist the temptation to collect or buy coral or shells. Aside from the ecological damage, taking home marine souvenirs depletes the beauty of a site and spoils other divers' enjoyment.

10. Ensure that you take home all your trash and any litter you may find as well. Plastics in particular pose a serious threat to marine life.

11. Resist the temptation to feed fish. You may disturb their normal eating habits, encourage aggressive behavior or feed them food that is detrimental to their health.

12. Minimize your disturbance of marine animals. Don't ride on the backs of turtles or manta rays as this can cause them great anxiety.

Marine Conservation Organizations

Coral reefs and oceans are facing unprecedented environmental pressures. The following groups are actively involved in promoting responsible diving practices, publicizing environmental marine threats, and lobbying for better policies.

CEDAM International
☎ 914-271-5365
www.cedam.org

CORAL: The Coral Reef Alliance
☎ 510-848-0110
www.coral.org

Coral Forest
☎ 415-788-REEF
www.blacktop.com/coralforest

Cousteau Society
☎ 757-523-9335
www.cousteausociety.org

National Coalition for Marine Conservation
☎ 703-777-0037
www.savethefish.org

ReefKeeper International
☎ 305-358-4600
www.reefkeeper.org

Reef Relief
☎ 309-294-3100
www.reefrelief.org

Surfrider Foundation
☎ 949-492-8170
www.surfrider.org

Listings

Telephone Calls

To call Hawaii or Midway Islands from outside of the U.S., dial the international access code of the country you are calling from + the area code for Hawaii (808) + the local 7-digit number. If you are calling from the U.S. mainland or inter-island, you need to dial 1 + the area code (808) + the local 7-digit number. Toll-free (800 or 888) numbers can be accessed only from the U.S., Canada and Guam: dial 1 + the area code (800 or 888) + the 7-digit toll-free number.

Accommodations

All of the main Hawaiian Islands, particularly Oahu, have a wide range of accommodations. You are bound to find something that suits your tastes and budget. For up-to-date information, contact the Hawaii Visitors and Convention Bureau.

Hawaii Visitors & Convention Bureau

The Hawaii Visitors and Convention Bureau offers a wealth of free information about each island in the state of Hawaii. Resources include up-to-date information on accommodations (from resorts to camping and everything in between), dining, activities, transportation, weather, a calendar of events and more. They offer a statewide travel guide (*The Islands of Aloha*) that is updated annually and can be accessed via their website (www.gohawaii.com). The website also includes island-specific information.

From the U.S. or Canada you can obtain general and statewide printed information by calling ☎ (800) GO-HAWAII, or island-specific information through the following numbers:

Oahu ☎ (888) 464-6665
Big Island ☎ (800) 648-2441
Maui ☎ (800) 525-6284
Lanai ☎ (800) 321-4666
Molokai ☎ (800) 800-6367
Kauai ☎ (800) 262-1400

From all other countries, you can write to:
Hawaii Visitors and Convention Bureau
2270 Kalakawa Ave., Suite 801
Honolulu, HI 96815
☎ 923-1811 Fax: 922-8991

Reservations and information for Midway Islands are obtained through the Midway Phoenix Corporation, the private company that manages transportation to and accommodations on the island. They have an informative website at www.midwayphoenix.com, or you can contact a representative directly through:

Midway Phoenix Corporation
100 Phoenix Air Dr.
Cartersville, GA 30120
☎ (770) 387-2942 Toll free: ☎ (888) MIDWAY-1 Fax: (770) 386-3053
or on Midway:
☎ 599-5400 Fax: 599-2922

Camping

There are many campgrounds and cabins throughout Hawaii. Facilities are run by the National Park Service, the State Parks and Recreation Department (part of Hawaii's Department of Land and Natural Resources), or individual counties. A few campgrounds are privately owned and operated. Reservations and/or permits are required in most cases. The Hawaii Visitors and Convention Bureau provides information on most camping facilities.

For reservations and information on all of Hawaii's national parks, contact the National Park Service, Prince Kuhio Federal Building, Room 6305, 300 Ala Moana Blvd., Honolulu, HI 96813, ☎ 541-2693. Information and maps are available on the web through the National Park Service at www.nps.gov.

State park reservations and information can be obtained on the web at www.hawaii.gov/dlnr/dsp/dsp.html. To get a permit for a state campground, you can write or visit the Division of Parks, 1151 Punchbowl St., Room 131, Honolulu, HI 96813, ☎ 587-0300, Fax: 587-0311; office hours are 8am to 3:30pm Monday through Friday.

You can also call one of the following state park regional offices:

Oahu ☎ 587-0300	Maui ☎ 984-8109
Big Island ☎ 947-6200	Kauai ☎ 274-3444

Diving Services

There are countless diving services available throughout the Hawaiian Islands. New services emerge, dive shops change owners, and sometimes shops will close. The following is a broad (but not exhaustive) list of services available in each of the regions covered in this guide. Mailing addresses are provided for contact purposes. Contact the dive shops directly for locations and specific services.

Most offer a range of rental and retail gear, airfills and guided shore and/or boat dives. Many offer certification and advanced diving classes and will accept Open Water referrals. All facilities should display their appropriate affiliations (NAUI, PADI, SSI, etc.). Most major credit cards are accepted.

Oahu

Aaron's Dive Shops
602 Kailua Rd.
Kailua, HI 96734
☎ 262-2333 Fax: 262-4158

Adventure Dive Hawaii, Inc.
P.O. Box 78
Kailua, HI 96734
☎/Fax: 235-4217

Alii Divers
24 Sand Island Access Rd.
Honolulu, HI 96719
☎ 843-2882

Aloha Dive Shop
Koko Marina Shopping Center
Hawaii Kai
Honolulu, HI 96825
☎/Fax: 395-8882

Atlantis Reef Divers
252 Paoa Pl., Rm. 2-2
Honolulu, HI 96815
☎ 973-1295
Toll free: ☎ (800) 544-6267
Fax: 973-1298

Beach Divers Hawaii, Inc.
4224 Waialae Ave., Suite 1A
Honolulu, HI 96816
☎ 737-7966 or 535-2487
Fax: 373-5329

Breeze Hawaii Diving Adventures
3014 Kaimuki Ave.
Honolulu, HI 96816
☎ 735-1857 or 735-1360
Fax: 737-4736

Captain Bruce's Scuba Charters
994 Waihole St.
Honolulu, HI 96821
☎ 373-3590
Toll free: ☎ (800) 535-2487
Fax: 373-5329
info@captainbruce.com
www.captainbruce.com

Dan's Dive Shop
660 Ala Moana Blvd.
Honolulu, HI 96813
☎ 536-6181 Fax: 536-6185

Diamond's Diving Tours
98-360 Koauka Loop #235
Aiea, HI 96701
☎ 488-9695

The Dive Authority
333 Ward Ave.
Honolulu, HI 96814
☎ 596-PADI
Toll free: ☎ (800) 808-DIVE

Dive Waikiki
2055 Kalia Rd.
Honolulu, HI 96815
☎ 949-3483

Diver's Edge
1155 Forte St. Mall #322
Honolulu, HI 96813
☎ 949-0373 Fax: 523-7988
godive@gte.net

East West Adventures
44-535 Kaneohe Bay Dr.
Kaneohe, HI 96744
☎ 236-2143

Elite Adventures Hawaii
92-914 Welo St. #76
Kapolei, HI 96707
☎ 672-3035 Fax: 689-3748

Fantasea Island Diving
345 Hahani St.
Kailua, HI 96734
☎ 262-2318 Fax: 262-4574
fid@pixi.com
www.qpg.com/F/fantasea

Hawaii 4 Divers, Inc.
94-1004 Puana St.
Waipahu, HI 96797
☎ 677-7237
Toll free: ☎ (800) 808-DIVE
Fax: 676-0565

Island Dive Center
670 Auahi St., Suite A1
Honolulu, HI 96813
☎ 523-9497 Fax: 523-9498
island@lava.net

Mahi Divers
85-371 Farrington Hwy.
Waianae, HI 96813
☎ 677-7975
Toll free: ☎ (800) 808-DIVE
Fax: 676-0565
info@oceanconcepts.com
www.oceanconcepts.com

North Shore Diving Headquarters
66-456 Kamehameha Hwy.
Haleiwa, HI 96712
☎ 637-7946
Toll free: ☎ (800) 578-3992
Fax: 637-8667
scuba@poi.net
www.ecstasea.com or
www.rebreathers.com

Pacific Diving Adventures
P.O. Box 4971
Kaneohe, HI 96744
☎ 235-9453 Fax: 235-9407
pacdive@poi.net
www.diveoahu.com

Paradise Divers
2375 Ala Wai Blvd.
Honolulu, HI 96815
☎ 921-3230 Fax: 921-3230

Snuba Tours of Oahu
172 Nawiliwili St.
Hawaii Kai, HI 96825
☎ 396-6169
Toll free: ☎ (800) 253-6163
Fax: 396-1150

Sun Divers Aquatics
P.O. Box 88732
Honolulu, HI 96830
☎ 924-8522

Sunshine Scuba
642 Cooke St.
Honolulu, HI 96813
☎ 545-5865 Fax: 545-5938

Vehon Diving Ventures
377 Keahole St.
Honolulu, HI 96825
☎ 396-9738 Fax: 395-7933
vehon@pixi.com

Waikiki Dive Locker
3027 Pualei Cr. #302
Honolulu, HI 96826
☎ 926-5008 or 923-0711
Fax: 922-4569

Waikiki Diving Center
1734 Kalakaua Ave.
Honolulu, HI 96826
☎ 955-5151 Fax: 955-6766

West Beach Dive Center
87-680 Farrington Hwy., Suite 200
Waianae, HI 96792
☎ 668-1616 Fax: 668-1567
wbdchawaii@aol.com
www.alternative-hawaii.com/wbdc

Windward Dive Center
789 Kailua Rd.
Kailua, HI 96734
☎ 263-2311 Fax: 262-8338
dive@divehawaii.com
www.divehawaii.com

Big Island

4 Wheel Divers
73-1143 Loloa Dr.
Kalaoa, HI 96740
☎ 325-3211
4whldvrs@gte.net

Aloha Dive Company
P.O. Box 4454
Kailua-Kona, HI 96740
☎ 325-5560
Toll free: ☎ (800) 708-KONA
Fax: 325-6688
diveadc@ilhawaii.net
www.alohadive.com

A Sea Paradise
P.O. Box 580
Kailua-Kona, HI 96740
☎ 322-2500
Toll free: ☎ (800) 322-5662
Fax: 322-2760
spscuba@interpac.net
www.seaparadise.com

Big Island Divers
75-5467 Kaiwi St., Suite 1
Kailua-Kona, HI 96740
☎ 329-6068
Toll free: ☎ (800) 488-6068
Fax: 326-5654

Body Glove Cruisers
P.O. Box 4523
Kailua-Kona, HI 96740
☎ 326-7122
Toll free: ☎ (800) 551-8911
Fax: 326-5654
www.bodyglovehawaii.com

Breeze Hawaii Diving (Kona)
74-5543 Kaiwi St., Suite 115
Kailua-Kona, HI 96740
☎ 326-4085 Fax: 329-4478

Dive Makai Charters
P.O. Box 2955
Kailua-Kona, HI 96745
☎ /Fax: 329-2025
www.divemakai.com

East Hawaii Divers
P.O. Box 2001
Pahoa, HI 96778
☎/Fax: 965-7840

Eco-Adventures Snorkel Surf & Dive
75-5744 Alii Dr.
Kailua-Kona, HI 96740
☎ 329-2323
Toll free: ☎ (800) 949-3483
Fax: 329-7091

Fair Wind
78-7130 Kaleiopapa St.
Kailua-Kona, HI 96740
☎ 322-2788 Fax: 324-1772
fairwind@interpac.net

Hawaiian Divers
660 Palani Dr., Suite P1
Kailua-Kona, HI 96740
☎ 329-2323
Toll free: ☎ (800) 525-2243
Fax: 329-2243

Hualalai Watersports
P.O. Box 383657
Waikoloa, HI 96738
☎ 325-8221 Fax: 325-8242
h2o-fun@aloha.net
www.dive-sunseeker.com/hualalai

Jack's Diving Locker
75-5819 Alii Dr.
Kailua-Kona, HI 96740
☎/Fax: 329-7585
Toll free: ☎ (800) 345-4807
divejdl@gte.net
www.divejdl.com

Kohala Divers Ltd.
Kawaihae Shopping Center
P.O. Box 44940
Kawaihae, HI 96743
☎ 882-7774 Fax: 882-1536
theboss@kohaladivers.com
www.kohaladivers.com

Kona Coast Divers
74-5614 Palani Rd.
Kailua-Kona, HI 96740
☎ 329-8802
Toll free: ☎ (800) KOA-DIVE
Fax: 329-5741
divekona@kona.net
www.konacoastdivers.com

Mauna Kea Divers
P.O. Box 44315
Kamuela, HI 96743
☎ 882-7730

Mauna Lani Sea Adventures, Inc.
68-1400 Maunalani Dr.
Kohala Coast, HI 96743
☎ 885-7883 Fax: 885-8848
winona@aloha.net

Nautilus Dive Center, Inc.
382 Kamehameha Ave. #102
Hilo, HI 96720
☎ 935-6939
nautilus@downtownhilo.com
www.downtownhilo.com/nautilus

Ocean Sports Waikoloa
69-275 Waikoloa Beach Dr.
Kohala Coast, HI 96743
☎ 885-5555 Fax: 885-5863
jjenet@interpac.net

Planet Ocean Watersports
200 Kanoelehua Ave, Unit 8
Hilo, HI 96720
☎ 935-7277 Fax: 933-1125

Rainbow Divers
P.O. Box 5554
Kailua-Kona, HI 96745
☎ 334-1154
Toll free: ☎ (800) 982-6747
Fax: 334-1158
rainbow@rainbowdiver.com
www.rainbowdiver.com

Red Sails Sports Hawaii
69-425 Waikoloa Beach Dr.
Waikoloa, HI 96743
☎ 886-2876 Fax: 885-4169
rsshi@gte.net
www.redsail.com

Sandwich Isle Divers
75-5729 Alii Dr., Suite 1
Kailua-Kona, HI 96740
☎ 329-9188

Toll free: ☎ (888) 743-3483
Fax: 326-5652
dive@sandwichisledivers.com
www.sandwichisledivers.com

Snuba Tours Big Island
P.O. Box 9020
Kailua-Kona, HI 96745
☎ 326-7446 Fax: 324-4719
snuba@ilhawaii.net
www.hshawaii.com

Maui

5 Star Scuba
Kaanapali Beach Hotel
Lahaina, HI 96761
☎ 667-5551 Fax: 661-0448

**Bill Dapuni's Snorkel
& Dive Adventure**
P.O. Box 1962
Kaunakakai, HI 9674
☎ 553-9867 Fax: 553-9009
cpgroup@aloha.net

Bill's Scuba Shack
2349 S. Kihei Rd.
Kihei, HI 96753
☎ 879-3483 Fax: 874-5606

Bob's Maui Dive Shop
Kapalua Shops
Kapalua, HI 96761
☎ 669-0484 Fax: 879-1644

Dive 4 Fun
P.O. Box 616
Kihei, HI 96753
☎ 879-3584 Fax: 874-1939

Dive Maui
900 Front St.
Lahaina, HI 96761
☎ 667-2080
offshore@maui.net

**Ed Robinson's Diving
Adventures/Kihei Scuba Services**
P.O. Box 616
Kihei, HI 96753
☎ 879-3584
Toll free: ☎ (800) 635-1273
Fax: 874-1939
infor@mauiscuba.com
www.maui.net/~robinson/erd1

Extended Horizons
P.O. Box 10785
Lahaina, HI 96761
☎ 667-0611
Toll free: ☎ (888) DIVE MAUI
Fax: 661-1896
scuba@maui.net
www.maui.net/~scuba

Fantasy Dives
P.O. Box 12381
Lahaina, HI 96761
☎/Fax: 667-5740

**Island Explorations
(Snorkeling Tours)**
P.O. Box 1107
Makawao, HI 96768
☎ 572-8437 Fax: 572-0769

Kaanapali Shores Beach Services
3445 Lower Honoapiilani Rd.
Lahaina 96761
☎ 878-6698 Fax: 878-3581

Lahaina Divers, Inc.
143 Dickenson St.
Lahaina, HI 96761
☎ 667-7496
Toll free: ☎ (800) 998-3483
Fax: 661-5195
lahdiver@maui.net
www.lahainadivers.com

Maui Diamond Seasports
P.O. Box 1599
Kihei, HI 96753
☎ 879-9119
Toll free: ☎ (888) 477-5484
diving@tiki.net
www.maui.net/~mcc

Maui Dive Shops
1455 S. Kikei Rd.
Kikei, HI 96753
Toll free: ☎ (800) 542-3483
mauidive@maui.net
www.mauidiveshop.com

Maui Diving Scuba Center
222 Papalaua St., Suite 112
Lahaina, HI 96761
☎ 667-0633
Toll free: ☎ (800) 959-7319
Fax: 667-5100
John@mauidiving.com
http://members.aol.com/div4me

Maui Sun Divers
P.O. Box 565
Kihei, HI 96753
☎ 879-3337 Fax: 879-3631
sundiver@maui.net
www.mauisundivers.com

Mike Severns Diving
P.O. Box 627
Kihei, HI 96753
☎ 879-6596 Fax: 874-6428
severns@mauigateway.com
www.severns.maui.hi.us

Pacific Dive Maui
150 Dickenson St.
Lahaina, HI 96761
☎ 667-5331 Fax: 667-6996
pacificdive@tiki.net
www.pacificdive.com

Reef Watchers
61 S. Kihei Rd., Suite A
Kihei, HI 96753
☎ 874-3467 Fax: 879-3696

Snuba Tours of Maui
485 Hoohalhala
Kihei, HI 96753
☎ 874-1001

The Scuba Connection, Inc.
4100 Ala Nui Dr.
Wailea, HI 96753
☎ 875-4100

Tropical Divers Maui
P.O. Box 11415
Lahaina, HI 96761
☎ 667-7709
Toll free: ☎ (800) 994-6284
Fax: 669-6284
getwet@maui.net
www.scubamaui.com

Kauai & Niihau

Blue Dolphin Charters, Ltd.
4331 Kauai Beach Dr.
Lihue, HI 96766
☎ 245-8681

Bubbles Below
6251 Hauaala Rd.
Kapaa, HI 96746
☎ 822-3483 Fax: 742-2258
kaimanu@aloha.net
www.aloha.net/~kaimanu

Dive Kauai Scuba Center
976 Kuhio Hwy. #C
Kapaa, HI 96746
☎ 822-0452
Toll free: ☎ (800) 828-3483
Fax: 823-6515
email@divekauai.com
www.divekauai.com

Fathom Five Divers
P.O. Box 907, 3450 Poipu Rd.
Koloa, HI 96756
☎ 742-6991
Toll free: ☎ (800) 972-3078

Fax: 332-0204
fathom5@fathom-five.com
fathom-five.com

Hanale Watersports
P.O. Box 3500-197
Princeville, HI 96722
☎ 826-7509 Fax: 926-1166

Mana Divers
P.O. Box 1137
Koloa, HI 96756
☎ 742-9303 Fax: 742-9849

Ocean Odyssey Dive Tours
P.O. Box 957
Lawai, HI 96765
☎ 742-6731 Fax: 742-9114

Sea Sport Divers
P.O. Box 638
Koloa, HI 96756
☎ 742-9303 Fax: 742-6636
seasport@pixi.com
www.kauaiscubadiving.com

Snorkel Bob's (Kauai)
4480 Ahukini Rd.
Lihue, HI 96766
☎ 245-9433

Snuba Tours of Kauai
1604 Papau Pl.
Kapaa, HI 96746
☎ 823-8912 Fax: 823-8912
snuba@aloha.net
www.hshawaii.com/kvp/snuba

Sunrise Scuba
P.O. Box 1255
Kapaa, HI 96746
☎ 822-7333
Toll free: ☎ (800) 695-DIVE
Fax: 823-6515

doctrox@aloha.net
www.sunrisediving.com

True Blue Charters & Ocean Sports
P.O. Box 1722
Lihue, HI 96766
☎ 246-6333 Fax: 246-6333
funkauai@hawaiian.net

Wet-N-Wonderful Ocean Sports
P.O. Box 840
Kapaa, HI 96746
☎ 822-0211 Fax: 822-8762
cnorman@aloha.net

Wet & Wonderful Watersports
4928-A Laipo Rd.
Kapaa, HI 96746
☎ 821-1599

Midway Islands

Midway Sport Diving, Inc.
P.O. Box 217
Newnan, GA 30264
Toll free: ☎ (888) BIG-ULUA
Fax: (770) 254-8329
dg@peachcity.com
www.midwaydive.com

Live-Aboards

Kona Aggressor II
Live/Dive Pacific, Inc.
Contact: 74-5588 Pawai Pl., Building F
Kailua-Kona, HI 96740
☎ 329-8182
Toll free: ☎ (800) 344-5662
Fax: 329-2628
livedive@compuserve.com
www.pac-aggressor.com
Home port: Kailua-Kona
Description: 80ft
Destinations: West coast of the Big Island
Season: All
Passengers: 10 (5 state rooms, queen and single bed in each, private shower and bath)
Other: 7-day trips (5½ dive days), 5 dives per day, onboard photo center and E-6 processing, handicapped accessible

Sunseeker
Contact: P.O. Box 383657
Waikoloa, HI 96738
☎ 325-8221 Fax: 325-8242
h2o-fun@aloha.net
www.dive-sunseeker.com
Home port: Kawaihae Harbor
Description: 53ft
Destinations: South Point to Waipio Valley on the Big Island
Season: All
Passengers: 4-6 (master suite and V-berth with private bathrooms)
Other: 1- to 7-day custom trips

Index
dive sites covered in this book appear in **bold** type

Lonely Planet Pisces Books

The **Diving & Snorkeling** guides cover top destinations worldwide. Beautifully illustrated with full-color photos throughout, the series explores the best diving and snorkeling areas and prepares divers for what to expect when they get there. Each site is described in detail, with information on suggested ability levels, depth, visibility and, of course, marine life. There's basic topside information as well for each destination.

Also check out dive guides to:

Australia: Southeast Coast

Bahamas: Family Islands
& Grand Bahama

Bahamas: Nassau
& New Providence

Bali & the Komodo Region

Bonaire

British Virgin Islands

Cocos Island

Curaçao

Fiji

Florida Keys

Jamaica

Northern California
& Monterey Peninsula

Pacific Northwest

Palau

Puerto Rico

Red Sea

Roatan & Honduras'
Bay Islands

Scotland

Seychelles

Southern California

St. Maarten, Saba,
& St. Eustatius

Texas

Truk Lagoon

Turks & Caicos

U.S. Virgin Islands

Vanuatu

Lonely Planet Series Descriptions

Lonely Planet **travel guides** explore a destination in depth with options to suit a range of budgets. With reliable, practical advice on getting around, restaurants and accommodations, these easy-to-use guides also include detailed maps, color photographs, extensive background material and coverage of sites both on and off the beaten track.

For budget travelers **shoestring guides** are the best single source of travel information covering an entire continent or large region. Written by experienced travelers these 'tried and true' classics offer reliable, first-hand advice on transportation, restaurants and accommodations, and insider tips for avoiding bureaucratic confusion and stretching money as far as possible.

City guides cover many of the world's great cities with full-color photographs throughout, front and back cover gatefold maps, and information for every traveler's budget and style. With information for business travelers, all the best places to eat and shop and itinerary suggestions for long and short-term visitors, city guides are a complete package.

Lonely Planet **phrasebooks** have essential words and phrases to help travelers communicate with the locals. With color tabs for quick reference, an extensive vocabulary, use of local scripts and easy-to-follow pronunciation instructions, these handy, pocket-sized language guides cover most situations a traveler is likely to encounter.

Lonely Planet **walking guides** cover some of the world's most exciting trails. With detailed route descriptions including degrees of difficulty and best times to go, reliable maps and extensive background information, these guides are an invaluable resource for both independent hikers and those in organized groups.

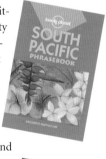

Lonely Planet **travel atlases** are thoroughly researched and fact-checked by the guidebook authors to ensure they complement the books. The handy format means none of the holes, wrinkles, tears or constant folding and refolding of flat maps. They include background information in five languages.

Journeys is a new series of travel literature that captures the spirit of a place, illuminates a culture, recounts an adventure and introduces a fascinating way of life. Written by a diverse group of writers, they are tales to read while on the road or at home in your favorite armchair.

Entertaining, independent and adventurous, Lonely Planet **videos** encourage the same approach to travel as the guidebooks. Currently broadcast throughout the world, this award-winning series features all original footage and music.

Where to Find Us . . .

Lonely Planet is known worldwide for publishing practical, reliable and no-nonsense travel information in our guides and on our website. The Lonely Planet list covers just about every accessible part of the world. Currently there are nine series: *Pisces books, travel guides, shoestring guides, walking guides, city guides, phrasebooks, audio packs, travel atlases* and *Journeys*–a unique collection of travel writing.

Lonely Planet Publications

Australia
P.O. Box 617, Hawthorn 3122, Victoria
☎ (03) 9819 1877 fax: (03) 9819 6459
email: talk2us@lonelyplanet.com.au

USA
150 Linden Street
Oakland, California 94607
☎ (510) 893 8555, (800) 275 8555
fax: (510) 893 8563
email: info@lonelyplanet.com

UK
10A Spring Place,
London NW5 3BH
☎ (0171) 428 4800 fax: (0171) 428 4828
email: go@lonelyplanet.co.uk

France
1 rue du Dahomey
75011 Paris
☎ 01 55 25 33 00 fax: 01 55 25 33 01
email: bip@lonelyplanet.fr

www.lonelyplanet.com